Faces of Hunger

D0914337

Studies in Applied Philosophy
edited by *Brenda Cohen and Anthony O'Hear*

Ethical Issues in Psychosurgery
John Kleinig

Madness and Reason
Jennifer Radden

Faces of Hunger
An Essay on Poverty, Justice and Development
Onora O'Neill

Non-Human Rights *
T. L. S. Sprigge

* in preparation

Faces of Hunger

An Essay on Poverty, Justice
and Development

Onora O'Neill
University of Essex

London
ALLEN & UNWIN
Boston   Sydney

Allen & Unwin (Publishers) Ltd,
40 Museum Street, London WC1A 1LU, UK

Allen & Unwin (Publishers) Ltd,
Park Lane, Hemel Hempstead, Herts HP2 4TE, UK

Allen & Unwin Inc.,
8 Winchester Place, Winchester, Mass. 01890, USA

Allen & Unwin (Australia) Ltd,
8 Napier Street, North Sydney, NSW 2060, Australia

First published in 1986

British Library Cataloguing in Publication Data

O'Neill, Onora
   Faces of hunger: an essay on poverty, justice and
   development.—(Studies in applied philosophy; 3)
1. Social justice   2. Justice (Philosophy)
I. Title II. Series
323.4'01   HM216
ISBN 0-04-170036-8
ISBN 0-04-170037-6 Pbk

Library of Congress Cataloging-in-Publication Data

O'Neill, Onora, 1941–
   Faces of hunger.
(Studies in applied philosophy; 3)
Bibliography: p.
Includes index.
   1. Social ethics. 2. Hunger. 3. Poverty.
I. Title. II. Series.
HM216.0456   1985   303   85-15053
ISBN 0-04-170036-8 (alk. paper)
ISBN 0-04-170037-6 (pbk. : alk. paper)

Set in 11 on 12 point Garamond by Paston Press, Norwich
and printed in Great Britain by Biddles Ltd, Guildford, Surrey

Editors' Preface

Studies in Applied Philosophy is intended to provide a focus for philosophical work which makes a positive and constructive contribution to contemporary debates in many areas of public life. In law, politics, economics, science, medicine and education, issues arise which have both ethical and philosophical dimensions. Each author approaches such issues from the critical and reflective standpoint characteristic of philosophy. The series is based on the belief that such an approach need not imply either moral ambivalence or an unwillingness to draw conclusions, and authors will in general defend a position and point of view; however, the purpose of the series will equally be served if a contribution provokes controversy or widespread assent.

Each volume will be of interest to students and teachers involved in academic and professional courses who wish to examine the philosophical and ethical assumptions made in their particular fields. At the same time, the series will interest students and teachers of philosophy who would like to see their own discipline provide a serious and constructive approach to matters of practical concern. By avoiding unnecessary technicalities, but without sacrificing rigour of argument, the books will also be accessible to the concerned general reader whose life is touched by the decisions of politicians and professionals, and who wishes to clarify the ethical arguments used or avoided in this process. We believe that *Studies in Applied Philosophy* will be of interest to all those concerned with the philosophical issues underlying debate and decision-making.

Brenda Cohen
Anthony O'Hear

Contents

Acknowledgements

I have been given a great deal of help in writing this book. My colleagues at the University of Essex carried added burdens during periods of my absence. The Research School of Social Sciences at the Australian National University and the Department of Philosophy at the University of Santa Clara welcomed me for 2 months apiece at early and late stages of writing. Different parts of the argument have been helped by numerous seminar discussions in Britain, in the USA and in Australia. My family and household have tolerated absences and abstraction over a long period. I have had constructive suggestions on many points in letters and conversations, and of the entire work from Rosemary Garvey, Steven Simmons, Brenda Cohen, Anthony O'Hear and Edward Nell. In addition to these five I would like to thank Tony Jackson, A. P. Williams and Susan Watkins; Jerry Schneewind, Arnulf Zweig and Henry West; Manuel Velasquez, George Lucas and Philip Alston; Philip Pettit, Stanley Benn, J. J. C. Smart and John Passmore; Marcia Baron, Arthur Caplan, Jim Nickel and Henry Shue; Ramaan Gillon, Richard Lindley and Keith Graham; Rosemary Sherratt, Adam Nell and Jacob Nell. The texture and focus of the book would have been very different without all their help.

Royalties from this book are assigned to Oxfam.

Preface

Towards the end of the twentieth century hunger and poverty no longer seem unalterable conditions of human life. Many societies of the temperate zones now have reasonable standards of life for all. Yet beyond the developed world destitution, hunger and soaring population growth persist and sometimes worsen.

Agreement that hunger and destitution should be ended is widespread, but often superficial. There is far more disagreement. Much of it is disagreement about *how* development can be achieved. Is food aid without development aid destructive? Is industrial or rural development more important? Are government policies or nongovernmental agencies more effective in bringing change? Does the working either of international agencies or of market forces promote or damage development? Is food self-sufficiency vital or irrelevant to development? Can population growth be slowed by family planning services and education? Or will it decline only when economic development is far advanced? Is development best pursued by aiming at economic transformation, or is it essential to aim for much wider, even revolutionary, social transformation? Does development require arms control and the release of funds now spent on weapons? These are a few of the broader questions debated in development studies.

This book will not try to resolve debates about *how* hunger and destitution can best be ended. Some of the deepest disagreements about world hunger and poverty are not about methods, but about *whether* and *why* those with the power to make fundamental changes ought to do so. Beyond the bland and superficial agreement that hunger and destitution should be ended, sceptical and self-seeking views are common. Poverty is indeed seen as a problem – for the poor. The rich and powerful often see no reason why they should help end distant poverty. This book asks *whether* and *why* development should be pursued, not only by the poor and vulnerable, but by the rich and powerful.

In asking these questions we run into huge difficulties. Much discussion of the ethics of poverty and development uses the standard modes of discourse of one or another social group or professional milieu. Each of these idioms presupposes categories and institutions which appear from other perspectives as problems rather than as premises for discussions of development, so seems to beg urgent questions. On the other hand more abstract ethical reasoning, which tries to transcend particular social contexts and categories, often seems blind to the urgencies of need and destitution and unconvincing to those who could change matters.

These difficulties appear in many places. The most common and respected sorts of secular ethical reasoning appeal to varied accounts either of human happiness or of human rights. Reasoning about happiness standardly takes beneficence as its central concern, and sees justice to the poor as no more than one of many aspects of beneficence. Reasoning about rights standardly makes justice its central concern, but interprets this as a matter of respect for a (fiercely disputed) set of universal rights, which may not mesh with human needs. Neither approach can readily show that meeting human needs is ethically fundamental. Both approaches are repeatedly hampered by the very abstraction from local context and categories on which they rely to reach an ideologically diverse audience. Discourse which is abstract enough to carry across social and ideological boundaries often carries no definite message.

Impatience with secular ethical reasoning is not only common, but very understandable. At present many who are eager to reduce poverty and destitution find the certainties of religious ethics, and in particular of liberation theology, a better guide to action that helps the poor. Others think that only the supposedly harder-headed professional discussion of development policies and possibilities is genuinely practical. Both these modes of thought in fact have heavy practical liabilities. Theological approaches assume a framework which limits communication with those who do not share the theology. Retreat to the 'practical' discourse of development studies suppresses but does not eliminate ethical assumptions. Disputes and failures of communication grow where fundamental assumptions are not shared. The costs may be slight with problems that are confined to the sphere of competence of a particular church or profession. Since hunger and poverty are global problems, however, their relief standardly requires communication between those whose categories and outlooks diverge. Retreat into the cosiness of shared tradition and rhetoric cannot resolve global predicaments.

Genuinely practical ethical discourse about world hunger and poverty needs modes of discourse and reasoning that do not presuppose the thinking of a theology or a profession, or other restricted outlook, yet are not too abstract to grasp questions of need directly. Without such reasoning, no amount of development expertise can prevent apathy, self-interest and failure of will from obstructing change. When those who have the power to change the lives of the poor see no reason to do so, little is likely to happen. In the last chapters of this book I have sketched a theory of obligation which can be used for deliberation that reaches beyond local idioms and outlooks and offers reasons why the powerful should help meet the needs of the distant poor. These reasons may, of course, be rejected or disregarded. Good reasons for action do not guarantee effective motivation; but discussion of good reasons for acting can nurture more effective motivation. The reasons for action to which I shall point conflict with the views of many theological, professional and political groups; but they can be understood and discussed by those with widely diverging ideologies.

The theory proposed here is mainly Kantian in origin and in aspiration, but is supplemented in two ways. First, it sees human beings not as abstract or ideal rational choosers, but as finite and vulnerable rational beings, who must take others' varied limitations into account when asking what obligations they have to others. Secondly, it includes a theory of ethical deliberation which suggests how we can move from abstract and widely understood principles of obligation to their determinate implications for particular situations.

Some will find this theory dubiously Kantian. It is distant in spirit from Kantian ethics as often taught and even more often rebutted. I shall say little here about reasons for reading the Kantian texts in this way. The aim of this book is to show that there are abstract and widely comprehensible principles, without which the activities even of partially rational beings risk incoherence, which have determinate implications for action that affects the hungry and destitute. If such a theory is plausible we have parts of an answer to the question of whether and why those with the power to do so ought to help meet the needs of others who are hungry and poor.

1
Applied Ethics and Uplifted Politics

> Above all, what about the world today? One third to one
> half of humanity are said to go to bed hungry every night. In
> the old stone age the fraction must have been smaller. This is
> the era of hunger unprecedented. (Sahlins, p. 36)

1 Hunger Unprecedented

Problems of poverty, hunger and famine are now as urgent as any
that could be faced. *Famines* have recently occurred in Bangladesh
in 1974; in Ethiopia both in 1972–74 and in 1984; in Cambodia in
the late 1970s and in the Sahel region of Africa in the early 1970s.
In 1985 Chad and the Sudan are threatened by famine and many
other African countries grow a decreasing proportion of the grain
that their rising populations need (Brandt, 1983, ch. 4; Dinham
and Hines, 1983; Hancock, 1985). In Asia and in Latin America
rising harvests have more frequently kept pace with or outstrip-
ped population growth, but often the poorest have not shared in
the improvements.

Beyond the epicentres of mass suffering, sporadic *starvation*
for some groups, regions or seasons is part of the normal cycle of
life in many of the poorer parts of the world. Starvation itself is
the most jagged evidence of *persisting destitution, endemic hunger
and malnutrition*. At a given moment in the modern world,
millions of human beings may be crushed by famines; but
hundreds of millions are unable to escape poverty and hunger
(Sen, 1981, ch. 4). Famine, starvation and persistent hunger all
take toll in human misery and mortality; the toll of famine is more
spectacular and intense, that of destitution more widespread and
persistent. Some past ages may have had a larger fraction of the

1

population living with hunger; but the number of hungry people has never been larger than it is today after decades of soaring population increases.

Another, and more political, description of the same realities would point to the dwindling numbers of grain-exporting countries, to the instability of grain prices, and to the increased dependence of the poorer parts of the world on grain grown in richer parts. It would also point to the lòw exports of many poor countries, to the falling prices the commodities that they often depend on now command and to their growing indebtedness (Morgan, 1979; Brandt, 1980, 1983; Dinham and Hines, 1983; IGBA, 1983). Whether food from the developed world is *sold* to the poor, as most of it is, or given in various forms of food aid, the result is dangerous dependence. In these conditions the sale or gift of food becomes a potent political weapon (Brown and Shue, 1977; Morgan, 1979, ch. 11; Wallerstein, 1980).

Problems that can be characterized in such differing terms are not only hard to end, but hard to think about in ways that do not come adrift. From the distance of the developed world these problems seem not just fearful and daunting, but often obscure and amorphous. It is hard to put a recognizable face on them or to know whose problems they are. A wild variety.of descriptions, prognoses and proposals is on offer, both in professional and in popular writing on economic and political aspects of world hunger and proposed remedies. Yet much systematic recent writing on distributive justice has had remarkably little to say about these global problems (Rawls, 1971; Nozick, 1974; Walzer, 1983). Much recent writing in ethics takes either beneficence or justice as fundamental, but assigns no special ethical importance to urgent need, to poverty or to hunger.

Disagreements begin with the very identification of the problem. Is the problem of world hunger that famine breaks out repeatedly? Is the appropriate response to provide emergency relief? Much of the publicity of famine relief organizations depicts hunger as episodic mass starvation, calling for the same sorts of immediate help and generosity that earthquake or flood victims need. Or is famine, like more scattered and less visible hunger, the critical symptom of social and economic structures that leave people in desperate poverty, which cannot be ended without fundamental and long-term changes?

Disagreements over the sorts of ethical problems raised by world hunger and poverty are equally basic. Is hunger a misfortune which calls for beneficence and help? The pervasive use of the term 'aid' to describe responses to hunger suggests as much. Or is ending distant hunger a matter of justice?

Since neither sort of disagreement can be easily resolved, this book is not anchored in a single well-charted debate. The topics it discusses have been buffeted by conflicting and turbulent social and intellectual currents. Sometimes the argument gained advantage from a particular tide of thought; sometimes it came closer to being swamped. The result is more polemical, more theoretical, rougher and less conclusive than anyone would wish. It hardly deserves the reassuring label of 'applied ethics'.

This disappointing result is not due to reluctance to reach definite and practical conclusions about ending famine, hunger and poverty. Conclusions are worth reaching only when we get there by ways that we can chart for others, and especially for others whose action or forbearance is demanded. The most elegant demonstrations do not lead far in practical affairs if we cannot show why the starting points they assume are worth taking seriously. Since practical reasoning about world hunger needs to address a vast and heterogeneous audience, it would be pointless to scurry to conclusions by routes which appear to be question-begging to parts of that audience. To reach beyond the audience of the like-minded may need a detour through more theoretical and reflective discussions – but the aim remains practical.

Some will think a theoretical approach slow and meandering, or even ineffective and irresponsible. If many are hungry and desperate what is there to do but provide food – at once? Those who put lives and livelihoods to the task of helping the destitute deserve admiration. Yet if hunger and poverty are not always sudden crises for which emergency measures are clearly appropriate, but are deeply rooted in human affairs, they may flourish more vigorously if cut back by inappropriate sorts of emergency intervention. Immediate action to reduce hunger or misery is (literally) vital; but it may be neither a complete nor a lasting *practical* response to hunger and poverty, or even to episodes of starvation and famine. If it is not clear what a sustained practical response demands, a theoretical approach is not prevarication.

2   Abstraction, Individualism and Applied Ethics

A theoretical approach can be of practical use only if it meets demanding standards. The contemporary movement in applied ethics has aimed to do so, and has generated a lot of optimism about prospects for introducing ethical deliberation into public affairs. Some writers think not only that 'applied ethics and uplifted politics ought to converge' (Hoffmann, 1981, p. 2), but that they have begun to do so, or will do so when further advanced (Ruddick, 1980; Parfit, 1984, pp. 453–454). Many point to the vivid contrast between the abstract and unpolitical character of ethical writing in the English-speaking world in the decades from G. E. Moore's *Principia Ethica* until John Rawls' *A Theory of Justice* (1971). In this period ethical writing was often preoccupied with the vicissitudes of personal life; in the past 15 years there has been much substantive, detailed and socially aware writing on problems of the public domain. These changes suggest that the positivist challenge to meaningful ethical discourse has finally been repulsed and that elaborated ethical theories and substantive arguments about handling specific cases can be introduced into the political arena.

However, there are unsettling features in this new ethical landscape. Two in particular seem serious obstacles to ethical deliberation which can have weight in public affairs. The first is still the 'abstract' character for which writing in ethics has so often been reproached. The second and equally familiar obstacle is that most ethical writing is still committed to the view that individual human beings are the only audience for ethical reasoning. Complaints that ethical theory is too individualist and too abstract are in no way new. They have been common coin for over a century. Many can be found in the writings of Burke, of Hegel and of Marx, or of other early critics of 'enlightened' ideas. The contemporary movement in applied ethics is one acknowledgement that ethical writing needs to be brought closer to deliberations of those involved in public affairs if it is not to seem remote, unrealistic or even sentimental.

The very use of the term 'applied ethics' is a claim that abstraction has now been banished. It suggests that we have a secure grasp both of adequate ethical theories and of an independent domain of data to which they apply. However, this engineering analogy does not fit well (Caplan, 1982). First, there are deep disputes about the adequacy of various ethical theories. Secondly, the presumed 'data' to which ethical theories might apply are themselves so theory-dependent that we cannot compare the ability of rival ethical theories to handle the same problems in coherent or convincing ways. The very features of an ethical landscape that loom largest in one theoretical vision may be invisible or deeply shadowed in the perspective of another theory. There are no ethically neutral descriptions of ethical landscapes. Perceptions as well as principles depend on theoretical perspectives and specifically upon ethical perspectives (O'Neill, 1984b, 1985a).

Nor do these problems begin at some supposed boundary of specifically ethical reflection and reasoning. Descriptions of human difficulties, predicaments and possible lines of action are ethically formed from a much earlier stage. The ways in which human action and situations are described and classified embody social and cultural assumptions. These are not neutral presuppositions shared by all ethical theories, but are often themselves matters of ethical substance and contention. In a broad domain of problems, such as those raised by world hunger and poverty, few problems can be picked out in ways that do not assume social, cultural and ultimately ethical commitments. Economic discussions that take centralized (or decentralized) decision-making for granted, or that assume some (but not other) property relationships, and social investigations that use (or shun) explanations in terms of class or ethnicity or the categories of action of those who are studied, embody substantive ethical assumptions. Development studies are filled with *ethical* as well as other disagreements over what the problems of development are and whose problems they are.

Abstraction cannot then be banished merely by conjoining ethical theory with the findings of development studies. We cannot expect economists, political analysts, famine relief experts and their like to show what 'the facts' of world hunger are, while experts in ethical theory show who may or must take which action. If the work of development experts embodies substantive ethical positions, neither their descriptions of problems nor their conclusions can be taken for granted in ethical deliberation. If the ethical positions assumed in development studies are submerged rather than critically developed we cannot do without ethical theory either. A mere *division* of intellectual tasks is not enough, because it will not show why one rather than another diagnosis of the problems of hunger and poverty and the possibilities for action should be accepted.

If the very 'data' which social inquiry provides for ethical deliberation presuppose ethical commitments, conclusions based on these data may beg crucial questions. However burning our desire for definite conclusions, however optimistic our claims on behalf of applied ethics, it will still be unclear what a nonabstract approach to ethics should be. Some of the more polemical parts of this book will suggest that various types of ethical reasoning reach determinate, action-guiding conclusions only by tacit and uncritical reliance on questionable accounts of world hunger and development. Some of the rougher and more tentative parts will suggest ways by which ethical deliberation might reach determinate conclusions without begging controversial questions.

The second major obstacle to fruitful ethical deliberation about problems of famine and world hunger is also familiar. Individualist assumptions persist in ethical theory, although it is widely acknowledged that individual action and efforts alone are unlikely to bring an end either to hunger or to poverty. Much ethical discussion assumes that we must make do either with patterns of reasoning that address only individual agents, or with those (such as certain forms of consequentialism) that apparently make minimal assumptions about agency. However, without an explicit view of agency we can hardly tell *to whom* ethical deliberation about problems of poverty and hunger should be addressed, or what form it must have to be accessible to its supposed audience. Undirected deliberation may not take us far in public affairs. Ethical considerations can address and reach the deliberations of institutions and collectivities,[1] as well as those of individuals, only if they emply a conception of agency which is not tied to individualism. Some of the more polemical parts of this book will probe and query various claims and disclaimers about agency; and some of the more tentative and theoretical parts will sketch ways of deliberating that allow for the agency not only of human individuals but also of some institutions and collectivities.

Unless we find ways of deliberating that can guide action and can speak not only to the individuals but to the institutions and collectivities which might make a difference, and do so without uncritical acceptance of received views of problems and of principles, there is no chance of applied ethics which converges with 'uplifted' politics. Without convergence, ethical reasoning about world hunger will either become sentimental rhetoric, or be assimilated into an established and establishment political (or other) agenda. If convergence is possible, ethical reasoning may be relevant not only for personal but for political deliberation. One central aim of this essay is to test the capacity of various modes of ethical reasoning to resist assimilation by established views without becoming irrelevant to public and political debate.

3   Deliberation, Ethics and Politics

Ethical reasoning which could criticize established practice, and yet was accessible to a full range of agents and of agencies, might provide a framework for fruitful practical deliberations about famine and hunger and their remedy. Such deliberation need neither accept established categories and views uncritically, nor be confined to lofty considerations that are remote and irrelevant (even incomprehensible) to those able to take action. It could speak not only to individuals but to influential institutions and collectivities. The aim of such deliberation would be wholly practical: but much of the preliminary work of charting such patterns of deliberation must be theoretical.

This book will try to deal with these preliminary, theoretical tasks without losing sight of the practical aim. Chapter 2 will look at some problems of world poverty and hunger, and at ways in which their very construal is ideologically – and ethically – contentious. Chapter 3 will sketch standards that ethical reasoning must meet if it is neither to be abstract, nor to accept established opinion uncritically, nor to be confined to an individualist framework. Chapters 4 to 7 will consider how well practical reasoning that focuses on results, on rights and on obligations, respectively, can meet these standards. The central skein of argument in these chapters concludes that a (maverick) Kantian theory of obligation comes closer to the standards of Chapter 3 than the currently popular consequentialist and rights theories.

Throughout, there will be comments on successes and difficulties that reasoning of each sort has encountered in discussion of hunger and poverty; but there will not be detailed prescriptions for dealing with particular predicaments of starvation and destitution. Prescriptions depend on critical scrutiny of actual situations and problems, without which deliberation and action are impossible. Actual deliberation about cases belongs only in a context of decision and action. If it is to be taken seriously it must attend to the technicalities of everything from monetary systems and trading agreements to those of agricultural and ecological research. Such deliberating can be found in scores of more-or-less specialized monographs. Accessible and quite detailed suggestions can be found in the two Reports of the Independent Commission on International Development Issues chaired by Willy Brandt (Brandt, 1980, 1983). Accounts of a wide variety of small-scale projects and innovations can be found in numerous more popular works (e.g. Harrison, 1983). Hence the lack of detailed prescriptions in this book is a token not of lingering abstraction, but of taking the practicality of ethical reasoning seriously. Serious ethical deliberation about problems of the public domain belongs only in contexts of action, including those of institutions and collectivities.

What philosophical inquiry can offer is a discussion of the urgency with which detailed recommendations should be viewed. Sometimes strongly held philosophical views can be obstacles to action. When influential philosophical writing depicts justice as a matter of not interfering with others' lives, and help to distant others as less weighty than justice, the claims of the hungry and poor are minimized and proposals for action may fall on deaf ears. Philosophical reflection is notoriously late on the intellectual scene, but it will not be redundant if it can show agents and agencies who affect poverty and hunger more urgent reasons to perceive and to treat the poor differently. That is the aim of this book.

Notes

1   The distinction intended here is roughly between institutions with more-or-less formalized information-gathering and decision-making capacities, and collectivities, which may share modes of thought, response and discourse, but often lack formalized procedures for inquiring, debating or making decisions. Bureaucracies, companies, nation states and government and international agencies are institutions; families, ethnic groups, occupational groups and classes may be collectivities. Membership in some collectivities coincides closely with membership in some institutions.

2
Distant Poverty and Hunger

Just about every commentator on the contemporary world
agrees that development is a problem. Some say that it is *the*
problem faced by humanity today. But what is 'a problem'?
Much of human life is unproblematic, in the sense that it
proceeds along lines that are familiar, even taken for granted.
. . . One man's problem may be another's inherent routine,
and vice versa. If one says that development is a problem, one
must follow this up with the question, '*Whose problem?*'
(Berger, 1974, p. 24)

Droughts may not be avoidable, but their effects can be.
(Sen, 1981, p. 123)

1 What Problems, Whose Problems?

Two conflicting intuitions may strike us as we begin to think
about ethical aspects of world hunger. One is that here things are
obvious. Hunger and famine are great evils, and their remedy,
available food, is entirely obvious. Both the problem and its
remedy are ethically uncontroversial.

The other and contrary intuition is that these problems and
their remedy escape the net of ethical thought, because they do
not arise from human misdeeds and cannot be remedied by
human action. Some claim that poverty and attendant hunger
arise mainly from geographical misfortune and natural catastrophe, so are beyond human responsibility or remedy. Others
claim that natural disasters (e.g. droughts, floods and earth-
quakes) often *precipitate* famine and hunger, but are not the
causes of either. Famine and hunger arise only when social and
economic structures are inadequate to absorb minor shocks or
natural disasters. If poverty and hunger, and even episodes of
famine, are seen as the results of complex social and economic

9

structures, their prevention or remedy will need changes in these structures. Here patterns of moral reflection may fail us. Most ethical thinking, theoretical and untheoretical, is at home in handling personal and interpersonal predicaments. It helps us to see how we may or should act towards particular others with whom our lives are shared, or with whom we interact, but it is silent about widespread evils and distant miseries whose remedy depends less on individual action than on changes in social and economic structures.

The difficulties of taking both of these lines of thought seriously show up long before we ask what should be *done* about famine and world hunger. Ethical deliberation begins with the identification of certain situations as problems, so in need of remedy or resolution. We can ask what should be done only when we know what sorts of problems world hunger raises, and whose problems they are.

It is difficult to see where a discussion of world hunger and famine, and of prospects for their remedy, can begin if perceptions and descriptions of poverty and development themselves embody ethical positions. Any starting point will seem arbitrary when there is not even an agreed listing of the problems in a domain. Depending on where we start and on the theoretical or ideological lens through which we look, some matters will appear in sharp focus and others will recede into the background or even become invisible. Problems may be seen in one perspective as wholly our own, but in another as problems for others of which we either may or must wash our hands. Even the most general accounts of a problem and its allocation can vary. Peter Berger (1974, p. 24) puts the predicament perceptively:

> Words describe the realities of human life. But they also have the power to create and shape realities. The words of the strong carry more weight than the words of the weak. Indeed, very often the weak describe themselves in the words coined by the strong. Over the last two centuries the strong have been the technologically advanced nations of the West. . . . It was they who named the others in a sort of negative baptism. Who were the others? When the West was still Christian in its outlook, the others were 'the heathen'. Then they became 'the uncivilized', or more optimistically 'the less civilized', as Western imperial power came to be

conceived of as a 'civilizing' mission. After the Second World War . . . the others began themselves to participate in the naming game. 'Underdeveloped countries' became 'developing countries'. Since the Bandung conference, in the mid 1950s the term 'Third World' has generated a mystique all its own. Although the ideological implications of these appellations were shifting . . . the basic empirical referents have not really changed. . : The basic division is between rich and poor

More recently, the blandly professional terms 'less' and 'least' developed countries have gained currency; these terms bracket deep disagreements about what development demands (Harrison, 1983, ch. 2). Since the Brandt Report of 1980 the involvement of the richer world in the problems of the poor has been stressed by using relational phrases such as 'North–South problems' or 'the North–South debate'.

Since we have to begin somewhere, I shall often use the blunt terms 'rich' and 'poor', but where more convenient will at least avoid the blander words of the strong by using the terms 'Third World' and 'North–South' to refer to a vastly heterogeneous group of countries and of problems, which may be linked only by poverty. I shall keep the term 'development' to refer to processes of change, which may be confined to economic growth, but may include profound transformations of life and outlook. By doing so the question of what development requires becomes a substantive ethical and social question, and not one to be prejudged by defining the term in a certain way. These terms do not suggest that the problems of the poorer parts of the world are evidently of one type. They do not imply that the problems of the poor are due to lack of Christianity or civility or polity, or of 'normal' economic achievement. It remains to consider what sorts of problems the poor of the world face, and whose problems they are.

One description of the problems of poverty and hunger takes the most extreme cases as paradigmatic. Famine and destitution are the ugliest and the most dramatic faces of poverty, and most likely to remind us of its harshness. These are the faces that we see in the publicity of international and voluntary organizations working for famine relief; but often enough the problem is not one of famine. Most present hunger and poverty do not kill by starvation, or reveal themselves in the listless suffering of migrating people. Hunger and poverty are the lot of hundreds of millions of our contemporaries; many of them may risk famine, but even in the worst of recent times most are not literally 'dying of hunger'. They are leading their ordinary lives; but these lives are short, harsh and insecure. The larger part of hunger is not dramatic. It shows itself in malnutrition, illness and expectations of life which remain obstinately low and is the core of persistent and desperate poverty. Famine episodes are only the tip of an iceberg whose invisible and larger part is endemic hunger and deprivation: not all the South is Ethiopia. If ethical deliberation about hunger and poverty is not to beg questions in its very identification of problems, the diversity of faces of famine and hunger must be acknowledged. Remedies appropriate for acute famine, such as food aid, may be useless or even harmful for those living whole lives on the edge of hunger (Jackson, 1982; Brandt, 1983, ch. 4).

Whether the problems of an area erupt in famine episodes, or whether they consist of grinding and persistent poverty, it is clear whose problems they are in the first place. Those who are poor and hungry cannot doubt what the problems are or that these problems are in large and harsh part theirs. Different faces of the problems may press closest at different moments. At one time it may be a poor harvest, lack of work or cash to buy food, or payment due to a landlord or a moneylender, at another an essential or unavoidable expense – a funeral, an illness, seeds or tools. Such problems arise within determinate contexts with a limited range of possible responses. Family and kinship networks may offer some but not other sorts of emergency support; loans may be available on certain terms and not on others; social insurance systems and aid organizations may (but most likely will not) offer certain types of assistance but not others. Begging, migration, crime and foraging may offer some meagre possibilities. When these remedies are inadequate those who suffer the problem must do without. At the limit poverty erupts into starvation and famine and some must do without food and live close to death. Hunger must be borne even when it destroys all energy needed for work; children must do without food needed for normal physical and intellectual growth; babies must die; curable illnesses must go uncured; herds must be slaughtered; crops and houses and land must be sold, however low the prices offered; families must migrate from familiar communities towards the faintest prospects of food or work. The times of emergency when such decisions must be faced and made offer few opportunities to ask whether the problem should be differently construed. Those who face these problems are powerless: if they were not, they would not face *these* problems. They may wish that the broader framework within which they have been brought to such a pass had been different; but they can do little about it. From their perspective whatever local 'rules of the game' determine descriptions of problems, expectations and options constitute the horizon of available action.

This does not mean that those who suffer or risk famine and acute poverty have no ethical problems. On the contrary, their problems are likely to be more searing and sharper than any faced outside emergencies. At close quarters it is all too clear what it does to deny growing children vital food or serious illness necessary treatment, or to sell the land or eat the seed without which food for future seasons is in question. The bitterness of such worse-than-Sartrian dilemmas is not that they cannot be decided by any moral code, but that they must be decided in terms of locally available options and codes. Those who make these choices face problems whose like many of us do not meet in a lifetime. To pass judgement on them, whether in terms of alien standards or their own, would only be offensive.

Anybody who reads this book will be distanced from such emergencies. Seeing hunger and poverty at a distance may lessen anguish, but can easily produce confusion rather than clarity. At a distance, views multiply. We may be unsure whose problem hunger is. Is it a problem *only* for those who risk or endure it, and have to cope with its results? Or is it also a problem for distant and richer others whose action might reduce – or exacerbate – the risks and suffering? If so is it a problem only for the rich of the same nation? Or is it an international problem? Is it a problem only for individual agents, or is it one for various collective and institutional agencies? Are some agents or agencies reponsible in part for producing famine and poverty, and what ought they to do if they are? Do responsibilities for ending famine, hunger and poverty belong entirely to the various international, national and voluntary agencies whose terms of reference mandate such action?[1] Or is a large part of the problem that some of these agencies are ill-adapted to many of their tasks (cf. Brandt, 1980, 1983; McNeill, 1981; Jackson, 1982; IGBA, 1983), so that the most fundamental need is to transform them? Who is responsible for such transformations? Should those at a distance see famine and the risk of famine as natural events, for whose relief and remedy they have no more responsibility than they might have for savage weather? Or can they see the problems of hunger and poverty as indeed responsive to human action, yet lying outside the domain of ethical reasoning or reflection, or at any rate outside the field of *their* ethical concern? Views from the centres of affluence may also simply obscure or hide rather than highlight serious miseries.

Answers to these questions depend in large part on a choice among perceptions of hunger and poverty as seen from a distance. Today distanced views of hunger and poverty are often views from the richer, developed world of poorer parts of the world. In large part they are views put forward by experts and officials: but expertise has not produced agreement. Despite claims to neutrality and objectivity, development experts disagree radically about how problems of world hunger should be described, whose problems they are, and what those who face these problems can or may or must do about them. Ethical deliberation about distant problems depends in the first place on understanding how variously these problems may be perceived and located from afar, and why some rather than other construals of problems should be taken as the basis for action. Without such understanding there is no context for deliberation, and none for action.

2   Famine and Hunger as Natural Disasters

There was a time when endemic hunger and episodes of famine may have seemed unavoidable natural hazards in human lives. When crops or hunting failed because of drought, or floods destroyed food supplies, or disease wiped out herds, there might simply not be enough food to go around. No matter that such disasters were usually local. Life was local and there was often no way to bring in food from far away. The only 'solutions' might be migration, with all its hazards, or enduring a lean season in which some would starve.

In this traditional picture famines appear as natural events, or perhaps (in a different metaphysical framework) as Acts of God, with catastrophic effects. All disasters may seem beyond human remedy to those who suffer them, and many beyond human responsibility. However, seen from afar it is much less clear that either famines or hunger are usually *natural* disasters. In the Anglican *Litany* famine is grouped with other scourges of mankind such as battle and murder. The intercession runs:

> From lightning and tempest; from plague, pestilence, and famine; from battle and murder, and from sudden death: *Good Lord, deliver us.*

May famines not, like battle and murder, be humanly produced, and perhaps human responsibilities? May they not be prevented or remedied by human action? Evidently enough, some famines are the result of human action. The results of siege or pillage, and of forced migration, are not natural but man-made disasters. So was the famine produced under the Pol Pot regime in Cambodia (Shawcross, 1984), but other hunger and famines do not seem to be due to any human action. We often hear that the Irish potato famine, and recent famines in Bangladesh and in the Sahel, and the famines of Ethiopia are due to crop failure, flood, drought or other natural events. Yet here too the spread and pattern of famine reflected the action and inaction of powerful agencies (Woodham-Smith, 1962; Franke and Chasin, 1979; Sen, 1981).

The view that famine and hunger are ultimately not produced or avertable by human action is put most forcefully in recent neo-Malthusian discussions of future famines that may be produced by the 'population bomb' of buoyant human fertility in a world of finite resources. Since neo-Malthusian thinkers often rely on a quasi-biological view of human motivation and action, they conclude that population growth is programmed to outstrip growth in resources, and that redistributive measures are doomed to be ineffective. (In this view they go beyond Malthus who thought population 'restraint' possible and that the minimum wage was socially rather than biologically determined (Malthus, 1798).) If these writers are correct, ethical reasoning, which is to the point only when action can make a difference, could have few implications for famine or hunger.

Even when famines *are* produced by natural disaster, or by the action of others who are impervious to reasoning, it is clear that their damage can be reduced and redirected by human action.

Even in the most traditional 'natural' famines, human activity has always made the difference between greater and lesser disaster. Prudent use of resources, like Joseph's, may stretch the surplus of fat years across lean seasons. The migration of hunters and pastoralists, the management of crops and of consumption, postponed marriage and the spacing of children have always made a difference. So too have more controversial practices: abortion and exposure of infants, hoarding and robbing, and corruption and extortion may make all the difference. Even when human activity cannot reduce the magnitude of a disaster, it has always been able to alter the distribution of suffering. Scarcity provides immediate opportunity for selfishness and for hoarding, for seeing that the worst effects of shortage are borne by others; it also provides opportunities to share and to save lives. Ethical questions can therefore be asked of *any* famine. They arise not from the mere fact of scarcity but from the possibility of reducing or magnifying its impact and modifying its distribution. Even when a famine is clearly attributable to natural events, those who hoard grain, or find their opportunity in others' desperation, as well as those who tighten their belts and share their food with most resolution, affect the distribution of famine. They may determine not only who is well- or ill-placed in the aftermath of famine, but also who survives.

This traditional picture has been altered by extended possibilities for intervening in distant famines. *Any* famine raises pressing problems for those immediately affected; *modern* famines raise questions for the far wider range of individuals, institutions and collectivities who *could* affect the course of famine. When life is not or need not be local, the range of possible interventions increases. Grain from the agricultural surplus of temperate zones can be taken to distant hungry regions. Modern medicine can rescue some whose starvation is advanced. Longer-term action to reduce the risk of further famines is also easier. Contraception makes family planning, even population planning, easier. Economic development can be pursued (or retarded) in multiple ways. Modern agriculture and food technology can yield and preserve far larger food supplies. Modern economic structures and transport can distribute food rapidly. Modern weather forecasting, irrigation and land-use can raise agricultural yields. At the least, modern famines *raise questions* for many more agents and agencies.

Persistent hunger which falls short of famine seems even less like a natural disaster which must be endured and cannot be averted. Yet some commentators on the persisting famine and hunger of modern times have seen both endemic hunger and its ultimate eruption into starvation and famine as natural disasters from which no modern technology provides escape. Neo-Malthusian lines of thought recur persistently, and were particularly prominent during the 1970s (Ehrlich, 1971; Meadows *et al.*, 1972; Hardin, 1974; Lucas and Ogletree, 1976). The metaphors used by these writers are striking. Each suggests an image of *uncontrollable* catastrophe: the growth of human populations is a 'bomb'; the peoples of the developed world live in a 'lifeboat', and can rescue others only at peril to all; the 'carrying capacity' of the planet earth is finite, and will only be damaged by over-use; the only responsible approach to world poverty must follow the military principle of 'triage', denying help not only to those who need none, but to the neediest also, who must be left to starve or survive as best they may while assistance goes only to the 'best risks'; like animal populations, human populations expand to fill available ecological niches and are unavoidably 'culled' by famine.

These vivid images all paint both famine and hunger (siege, pillage and the like apart) as natural disasters and as beyond human remedy. In these neo-Malthusian pictures, attempts to avert or reduce famines or hunger are seen as futile, even counter-productive. The suggestion is that while modern technology makes intervention in distant problems possible, it does not make them remediable. Intervention is meddlesome and likely to worsen the ultimate catastrophe. Sooner or later population growth will catch up with food supplies, however much these have been increased. Well-intentioned attempts to postpone the crunch only guarantee that there will be more human lives to be lost in the ultimate catastrophe.

These neo-Malthusian perspectives suggest that ethical reasoning about famine has a severely restricted task. The starkest claims insist that famine and hunger cannot be prevented, at least in the long run, and that attempts to intervene are likely to produce unsustainable population growth and so lead to more deaths. *Laissez faire* is then the only ethically responsible approach to problems of famine and hunger. Apparently modern achievements, which appear to widen human possibilities, have here widened only possibilities for harm.

Neo-Malthusian thinking has been challenged at many points. The most general challenge is to claims that famine and hunger must be seen as *natural* phenomena, hence beyond human control or ethical concern. The biological and crisis metaphors on which neo-Malthusians have depended are suspect (Hinds, 1976; Verghese, 1976; McCloskey, 1983, chs 2 and 3). Human populations are not doomed to increase to fill available ecological niches: many in the developed world have undergone a *demographic transition*, so reducing their fertility that they have little or no population growth in spite of long life expectation (Boserup, 1981; *People*, 1984). Population growth cannot be predicted by projecting present rates of increase to produce the fantasy of a world weighed down by living, starving humans. Projections yield predictions only when it is known that all other factors will be constant: and there is seldom reason to make that assumption in social or demographic matters. The earth is neither a finite pasture nor a lifeboat.

Another, more specific objection often made to neo-Malthusian claims is that the demographic transition in the now-developed countries was less a *precondition* than a *result* of economic growth. When poverty is greatest, infant mortality will be high and social security slight. Only those with large families can be sure that some children will survive. In the meantime the children of the poor begin work and contribute to their families early in life. The persistence of high fertility may then be a *rational* response to precarious social conditions. Once poverty is less and life less precarious, fertility can be expected to fall. This picture is partly confirmed by evidence of recent fertility declines in some more developed Third World countries (Mamdani, 1972; IGBA, 1983; *People*, 1984). If rapid population growth is no more inevitable in the underdeveloped world than it is in the now-developed world, famine and hunger are not unavoidable results of biological processes. They have been eliminated in some parts of the world. Can they then not be eliminated throughout the world? If they can be eliminated, should not ethical reasoning help us to see who should do what to bring this about?

Even if neo-Malthusian views of population growth were correct, they would not show that *laissez faire* policies towards distant famine and hunger were ethically required. Even in the most traditional settings, where distant remedies for hunger or famine were unavailable, their occurrence raised ethical problems.

Even when the magnitude of scarcity cannot be much altered, its distribution can be varied in many ways. Modern technical and social changes have not changed that, but have provided many *additional* ways to redistribute the impact and burden of famine. There are always questions about the distribution of suffering. We can always ask whether the full burden of scarcity should be borne where it first occurs, or should be more widely shared. Only if we create total scarcity – whether by following a Malthusian path (a possibility, even if not an inevitability) or by nuclear or other eco-catastrophe – need we face scarcity which can neither be mitigated nor redistributed. In the meantime, like those to whom only local remedies were available, we face questions about mitigating and distributing harm and suffering that arise. These questions may be less pressing, yet are often harder for us, in that action-at-a-social-distance opens so many possibilities, yet is both difficult and ill understood.

The persistence of biological, neo-Malthusian and other perspectives which see famine and hunger as natural and largely irremediable disasters is no doubt of deep sociological and psychological interest. Whether it reflects atavistic fatalism or the self-interest of those who have enough and want reasons not to help others who do not, or whether it contains a deep truth about the very long run is, however, beside the point. In the long run we shall all no doubt be dead: but if we construe the famines and hunger of today as natural and irremediable disasters, so impervious to human action, some of us will be dead much sooner and unnecessarily. The hunger of our day, as of past days, raises questions about distributions of benefits and burdens. Its impact has not been shown unmodifiable or its recurrence inevitable. There is opening enough for ethical deliberation about distant hunger even if the starkest neo-Malthusian views of population and resource growth are correct; if they are false such deliberation has an even wider range of tasks.

3   Social Structures of Famine and Hunger

Most non-Malthusian writing in development studies denies that famine and hunger are natural disasters. It usually depicts them as social rather than natural problems, produced by economic, political and ideological forces, rather than by biological and climatic constraints. Famines that are *solely* natural disasters, brought on by floods or droughts in regions too remote even for modern technologies to bring relief, are, by the nature of the case, rare in the modern world. Many recent famines have been due only in part to natural disasters (Shepherd, 1975; Franke and Chasin, 1979; Sen, 1981), and *endemic* hunger and poverty are always unlikely to be due to *episodic* disasters.

Today both famines and endemic hunger typically reflect a wide range of factors. Some famines occur even when locally available food is enough to meet needs, because social and economic structures leave the poor without either entitlement to food, or opportunity to earn such title (Sen, 1981). Even famines which are precipitated by natural events, such as floods or crop failure, might have been avoided if economic or political or other social circumstances had been different. It is often well known which regions risk famine and who is likely to need food. There are often no natural or technological obstacles to providing food to those who need it. Some floods and droughts may in the first place not be purely natural disasters, but may reflect investment – or lack of investment – in dams and erosion control. Some ecological damage that aggravates the risk of famine may reflect earlier economic choices, such as the development of plantation agriculture or the displacement of pastoralists by the introduction of cash-crop farming on former grazing lands (Franke and Chasin, 1979; Sen, 1981; Jackson, 1982; Dinham and Hines, 1983).

A comparison with some natural hazards of life in the colder and richer North is suggestive. The harshness of northern winters would cause countless deaths annually if this was not averted by social and economic structures which provide at least adequate clothes, shelter and heating for all. Such deaths are not now seen as inevitable natural disasters, although that is what they would be if the North had only the technology and social system of the Dark Ages. Similarly, the infertile soils and variable rains of various parts of the South would not make high death rates inevitable if appropriate social and technological changes could be made.

Yet if many famines and all persistent hunger are attributed to social structures rather than to natural disasters, their remedy may once again be thought immune to ethical reasoning. Fundamental economic and social structures are not easily changed, least of all by individual decisions. Yet ethical reasoning is often thought relevant only to individual decisions and so unable to address problems of famine and persistent poverty. There are endless examples of trends and patterns which are not due to individual decisions. Demographic trends reflect not only parents' 'reproductive decisions' but more fundamental underlying social and economic conditions. Even if contraceptive technology is available, family size may remain high when economic conditions are precarious and many mouths also provide cheap labour and the rudiments of a welfare network (Mamdani, 1972; Boserup, 1981). Migration to the shanty towns of the Third World may reflect not only the 'economic decisions' of those who move, but disruptions of subsistence agriculture by various sorts of economic change, including the provision of food aid in ways which destroy traditional markets for local farmers (Jackson, 1982; Dinham and Hines, 1983). If ethical reasoning only addresses individual 'decision-makers', it will be irrelevant in debates about changing the social and economic structures within which decisions are taken. Relief and development policies would have to take account of economic and social considerations but could leave ethical debate aside.

There would still be plenty to debate. Non-Malthusian writers agree that famine and persistent poverty rarely result from natural causes alone – but they disagree fiercely over the shape and description of these problems and whose problems they are. As a result there are also sharp disagreements about available and preferable remedies. There are also some points of agreement. For example, very few disagree with Sen's point (1981, p. 97) that

> no matter how a *famine* is caused, methods of *breaking* it call for a large supply of food in the public distribution system.

There is also general agreement that persistent poverty needs *development* rather than *relief* and that this is remarkably hard. Although world hunger is not a natural disaster, the 'mechanisms' of markets and the 'dynamics' of social forces make it an intractable range of problems.

A main and recurring centre of dispute is between advocates of growth-oriented development strategies, both capitalist and socialist, and their critics. Advocates of growth have frequently held that the development of a modern, usually industrial, sector in a backward economy will lead to economic development. The varied critics of such views doubt that growth alone will be enough, and typically think that distributive questions too must be tackled if famine and extremes of poverty are to be overcome. On either view the reduction and remedy of hunger and poverty demand enormous economic and political changes.

None of the parties to these debates claims that growth without appropriate distribution or appropriate distribution without growth could solve the problems of world poverty and hunger. It is rather that their emphasis is different. The advocates of growth see the first moves to end poverty as *investment* in poor countries. Investment may be funded by development loans from international agencies, such as the World Bank, which makes loans both at commercial rates of interest and at lower 'soft' rates through the International Development Association; by capital borrowed on international financial markets; by bilateral loans from particular richer countries; or directly by investment by transnational corporations (Brandt, 1980, chs 11–15). Advocates of growth also stress the importance of trade agreements which provide poor countries with some tariff protection, while securing access to export markets (Brandt, 1980, ch. 11). The hope is that investment, coupled with some agricultural innovation, can fuel economic growth, and that ultimately the benefits of this growth will 'trickle down' to the poorest so that famine, the risk of famine and lesser but persistent hunger will end.

Critics of growth-oriented development strategies point to various difficulties. Growth rates in poor countries have often been high; but so has population increase. A rising level of Gross National Product does not guarantee that average income will rise, since population may rise faster; and a rise in average income does not guarantee that the number who are destitute will fall, since the rise may be unevenly distributed. An expanding economy may also be one with shrinking average expectations or with shrinking or static expectations for an increasing number. Agricultural production in many developing countries has been on the rise since 1950; yet cereal imports have also grown throughout this period (Brandt, 1980, p. 91). Fewer and fewer poor countries can grow the food they need. A focus on aggregate figures and on growth, rather than on distribution, can obscure persisting poverty. Even if a demographic transition is now beginning in the Third World, the roll-on effect of the births of the last 20 years guarantees staggering increases in population in many countries for the next few decades (Brandt, 1980, ch. 6).

The pessimistic view of the critics of growth-oriented develop-ment strategies is that much growth in the Third World has benefited small 'enclave' economies, producing a modern, usually urban, sector which neglects, even worsens, the lives of the rural poor, so leading some of them to leave the land and settle in the shanty towns which mushroom on the edges of Third-World cities. The profits from the developed sector may go to repay the high interest on development loans, or leave the country when transferred by transnational corporations, or be used to import luxuries for local elites, or to buy arms. They seldom benefit the really poor. The real sources of persistent hunger and destitution are then seen as being as much political as economic. An interna-tional economic system which apportions investment and even development loans mainly on the basis of expected profitability and other commercial criteria, far from ensuring a transformation of the lives of the poorest, may secure and endorse the position of the relatively powerful. Action confined by existing economic structures will then not be enough; problems of hunger and poverty will need radical political change.

Some critics of growth-oriented policies have offered as models of relatively successful intervention certain very small scale, 'bottom up' initiatives undertaken mainly by voluntary organiz-ations, which have made efforts to involve and mobilize the poor themselves, and have avoided reliance on large infusions of outside capital (Schumacher, 1973; McNeill, 1981; Jackson, 1982; Kitching, 1982; Harrison, 1983). Some of these schemes, it is claimed, avoid hazards such as the diversion of benefits to those who are best off (whether local elites or Third-World govern-ments or transnational corporations). The successes of such projects are encouraging; but they can hardly provide a general approach to development. Small may be beautiful, but when the problem is vast small may be inadequate. The very social and technological features which have made some small-scale projects successful may not survive being scaled up to deal with larger problems. Nor can small projects and remedies change economic and political structures or alter the terms of trade or the grip of international financial institutions. Local initiatives can be swamped by the tides of market forces.

Other critics of growth-oriented development have advocated political changes which secure greater independence from the developed world and its possibly inappropriate forms of technology and economic organization. Some writers see the persistence of neo-colonialism as the major difficulty of the Third World (Frank, 1969; Kitching, 1982). Without dependence on capital investment and aid from the developed world and resulting vulnerability to more powerful economic forces, the benefits of development would be more likely to reach those who need them. Yet this sort of economic independence has enormous costs. It refuses what may be the best or only sources of capital investment, and may undercut access to export markets. Policies which aim only at *national* economic autonomy may reduce the possibility of economic domination by other countries or by transnational corporations, but cannot guarantee a distribution of benefits which helps the hungriest and neediest. Nation states are not the unit of poverty.

Yet other critics of growth-oriented development are eager to see more radical and political changes, which not only secure national economic independence but establish economic structures that can end abject poverty. They point to the more successful aspects of societies – such as Cuba or China – where the fruits of revolution include the ending of acute hunger. Not every revolution guarantees such results, or even such priorities; but on some views *only* a revolution – the right revolution, which not only rejects existing economic structures but relies on various forms of popular mobilization – can produce such changes.

Growth-oriented approaches to poverty and hunger see them as problems for existing economic institutions and forces, to be handled in the main by market forces operating within confines defined by national governments and international institutions. Distribution-oriented approaches tend to see them as problems for present and future political institutions and forces. Neither approach appears to leave much room for specifically *ethical* deliberation about world hunger. If famine and hunger are produced by social and economic structures, and will lessen only when these structures are changed, change may seem beyond the scope of ethical deliberation. Indeed, if ethical deliberation addresses only *individual* agents, and depends upon a conception of agency unique to human individuals, must not development policy and decisions be a matter for economic and political but not for ethical deliberation?

However, since development policies and decisions are practical matters and so need deliberation, they too must allow for *some* form of agency. Social or economic analysis which depicts famine and endemic hunger as wholly governed by economic and political structures and processes, beyond all action or intervention, leaves no more foothold for deliberation than do neo-Malthusian analyses which depict them as biologically determined. Deliberations about development might be addressed to various sorts of agents and agencies. If they can be directed only to individual agents, then ethical deliberation is no more restricted in scope than are other sorts of deliberation; if they can also be addressed to certain institutions and collectivities, then there are at least some agencies other than individuals to whom ethical deliberation too might be addressed.

Yet this seemingly straightforward view of agency and of ethical deliberation is often rejected. It is commonly assumed that many agents and agencies are capable of deliberation about policy and economic issues, yet incapable of ethical deliberation. A long tradition excludes the public domain and decisions made in it from ethical demands. Sometimes reasons are given for this exclusion: for example, ethical language is said to be discontinuous with descriptive or factual language. On a certain view of the matter this allows for agencies who engage in political or economic deliberation, which depends closely on 'factual' uses of language, but are incapable of ethical deliberation. This is no time to rehearse these protracted debates. Their persistence is not good evidence for any fundamental distinction between the language of values and the language of facts (Rorty, 1983). Unless and until the distinction is uncontroversially established, there are no sufficient reasons for assuming that one sort of practical deliberation is the exclusive preserve of individual agents. Ethical deliberation about problems of famine and hunger may then be possible not only for individual agents but for institutions and collectivities which deliberate in other ways about public affairs.

Modes of thought which place problems of famine and persistent hunger not only far away, but beyond the reach of ethical deliberation, may be not so much neutral and objective as distanced and dissociated. These modes of thought include social and economic and biological theories which place distant famine and hunger beyond the limits of human action and intervention, and see them as unalterable features of human landscapes rather than as practical problems. They also include social and ethical theories which allow that famine and hunger are practical problems which action may change, but see them as posing ethical problems only for individuals. Since different views of the problems of famine and hunger reflect the varying lenses of social and ethical theories, a critical assessment of these images must look at the theoretical instruments that shape them. Paradoxically, a *theoretical* turn is needed if famine and hunger are to be seen as *practical* problems, and also if we are to determine what sorts of practical problems they raise. Only by seeing how questions of famine, hunger and development appear through the lenses of various ethical theories can we discover whether they raise *ethical* problems which can be grasped and tackled not only by individual sufferers and their individual sympathizers, but by a larger range of agents and agencies whose deliberation and action could make a difference.

Note

1   The range of agencies whose mandate requires action that affects the prospects of the poor is enormous. The *global, international* organizations whose influence is most pervasive include the International Monetary Fund (IMF) (which regulates the international monetary system), the General Agreement on Tariffs and Trades (GATT) (which aims at liberalization and stabilization of terms of world trade), The World Bank (and its affiliates) which make development loans, as well as many of the United Nations organizations, such as UNCTAD, WHO, FAO, UNICEF and UNHCR. The FAO (Food and Agriculture Organization) runs the World Food Programme (WFP). Other *regional international* agencies that affect development include the European Economic Community (EEC), and the Organization of Petroleum Exporting Countries (OPEC). In addition, richer countries have their own development and aid agencies, such as the US Agency for International Development (AID) or the UK Overseas Development Administration (ODA), while the entire governmental structure of poor countries affects the prospects of their people. Finally, there are many *voluntary* Non-Governmental Organizations (NGOs). Some of the best known ones are OXFAM, CARE and CRS. Accessible accounts of this gamut of agencies, varied criticisms of their effectiveness, and suggestions for restructuring can be found in Brand (1980, 1983), McNeill (1981), Jackson (1982) and IGBA (1983).

3

Standards for Practical Reasoning

> We are for ever hearing sermons about what ought to be done from people who do not consider whether what they preach can be done. As a result the exhortations, which are tautological reiterations of the rule which everybody knows already, prove terribly boring. (Kant, 1924, p. 3)

1 Practical Reasoning and Abstraction

It is often a waste of time to reason with others of different or distant outlook. If we are lucky and find enough agreement for collaboration or coordination, it may be pointless to try to resolve disagreements, by reasoning, or by any other method. However, the case for leaving disagreements unresolved lapses when they are an obstacle to action, as with many disagreements over hunger and poverty. Disagreement about the possibility of challenging or changing social and economic structures which provide inadequate entitlements to food or income for many are not trivial. Nor are disagreements between those who see action to help the hungry as an optional matter of generosity and those who see it as an urgent matter of justice.

Such disagreements can only be resolved by reasoning that is *accessible* to those who disagree and sufficiently powerful to *guide action* by discriminating between ethically significant categories. Ethical reasoning cannot be *practical* unless it takes account of the variety of agents and agencies whose action will actually affect the incidence and severity of famine and hunger, and of the varied grids of categories to which these agents and agencies attend. But accessibility alone is not enough. *Practical* reasoning also needs patterns of argument that can show which actions are ethically required or forbidden, commendable or reprehensible. Plenty of supposedly ethical reasoning does not

27

meet these standards. Instead of genuine practical and political deliberation we find worthy rhetoric appealing to unspecified agents. Unless we can find modes of reasoning that are accessible to actual agents and agencies, and can guide their acting, ethical deliberation cannot be genuinely practical.

However, there is a danger in insisting on *accessible* practical reasoning. What makes reasoning accessible to one or another agent or agency is that it uses categories familiar to that agent or agency. However, restriction to those categories may tie ethical reasoning to locally accepted ethical and other views. An initial view suggests that ethical reasoning can either be *accessible* to established agents and agencies or *critical* of the established practices of these agents and agencies, but not both. Yet adequate practical reasoning needs to be both accessible and critical.

One traditional approach to this dilemma has been to rely on ethical reasoning that takes an *abstract* view of agents and agencies and their categories, so can appeal to a wide audience. A consideration of the merits and difficulties of abstract views of agency is therefore a natural first step in discussing standards of practical reasoning. Yet no criticism of ethical theory has been more frequent or popular than the claim that it is just too abstract to guide action. The whole intellectual spectrum from Marx to Bentham down to their least significant followers urges this point. It is a curious criticism.

A theory or principle is abstract if it gives a general account of some matter – one that literally abstracts from details so is (more or less) indeterminate. All descriptions and prescriptions, indeed all uses of language and reason, must be to some extent abstract; they cannot be as determinate as the states of affairs or actions that satisfy them. The problem with ethical theory cannot then be just that it is abstract, since this would be a problem of all domains of discourse.

Perhaps then the problem with ethical theory and principles is that they are *too* abstract, that too much is left out. This also is a curious criticism. *All* theories and principles and most descriptions must abstract from most details and circumstances. Why should ethical theory in particular be criticized for abstraction when other abstract theories or principles or description (such as scientific theories, legal principles and commercial descriptions) are just as abstract, yet capable of guiding engineering or legal or accounting practice?

Is the problem that too little attention is paid to the process of applying ethical theories or principles? The claim is plausible. A good deal of twentieth-century ethical writing has paid little attention to the 'minor premises' of ethical reasoning, and has skirted traditional Aristotelian and Kantian topics such as the nature of deliberation, judgement and casuistry, which do consider ways in which situations and problems are picked out for adjudication or resolution in terms of some ethical theory or principle (Wiggins, 1975–6; Beiner, 1983; O'Neill, 1985a). Too often, even in writing in 'applied' ethics, which is specifically committed to reasoning which can guide action, ethical problems are seen as unproblematically there in the world, problems that 'crop up' and can be confronted by any of a variety of possibly adequate ethical theories. If ethical problems are themselves theoretically structured this is not an adequate picture of the application of ethical theories. Problems are antecedently given only in text books. In contexts of action questions are begged (usually in favour of received views) if some 'obvious' account of a problem or an area of life is taken for granted. In ethical deliberation, as elsewhere, it matters who controls the agenda. An adequate account of reasoning that can guide action must include not only principles of action (the major premises) but an account of judgement which explains why particular situations should be grasped under one rather than another possible description (the minor premises).

However, many of the critics of ethical theory who have complained that it is too abstract may not have meant only that it needs to be supplemented with an appropriate account of judgement. That could perhaps be remedied, so would not be a disastrous failing. What they have in mind seems often to be that ethical theories are not only *abstract* but *idealized*. Any useful description or principle has to leave out many details, so will be abstract. However, selective *omission* is not the same as selective *addition*. Selective addition may render a theory inapplicable to the domain for which it is intended. Theories are not so much abstract as idealized if they rely on descriptions or principles which augment and 'streamline' those which apply to the situations and actions which are taken to fit the theory. Such selective idealization is particularly evident in the accounts of agency on which much ethical reasoning relies.

Many theories of rational choice, for example, do not simply abstract from actual features of human choosing and reasoning capacities, but rather introduce idealized conceptions of rationality which are standardly absent, and often not approximated, in human choosing. Such theories do not provide a particularly abstract account of human choice, but rather an inaccurate and (at best) approximate and (at worst) misleading account of human choice. Ethical deliberation which starts with principles and theories which are not just abstract but distorting idealizations of some situation may be inappropriate for guiding action (they may have other, theoretical uses). Unfortunately, many ethical theories take idealized views of deliberating capacities. When they do the prospects for applied ethics are dim. However noble and lofty the rhetoric, the theory may be an obstacle to laying hands on any context of action. We may be left echoing Peguy's succinct summary of a whole tradition of (probably unfair) comment on Kant: 'Le kantisme a les mains pures, *mais il n'a pas de mains*' (Peguy, 1910). Actual practical deliberation must get its hands on the matter to be dealt with.

2   Reasoning Across Boundaries

Most practical reasoning takes a specific social and ideological context for granted. Legal reasoning takes places in contexts which define certain problems (crimes, cases or processes), certain agents and agencies (counsel, judges, courts or juries) as well as specifying principles to be followed (laws or rules of procedure). Commercial reasoning assumes a context of problems (available opportunities to buy or sell, produce, work or invest), a cast of agents and agencies (purchasers, vendors, workers, employers, firms and banks) as well as specifying principles that are to be followed (accepted forms of bargaining and contracting). Specifically ethical reasoning may not be analogous.

Much of our daily, 'normal' ethical reasoning assumes a range of problems, of agents and agencies and of accepted principles. In deciding how to deal with a pressing debt a poor farmer may consider that the only available options are a loan from relatives or a moneylender, or the sale of land. The description of the problem – a debt for which there are no funds to hand – is taken for granted. So is the cast of relevant agents and agencies: the farmer, the relatives, the money lender, possible purchasers. So are the possible principles of action: paying up, reneguing and taking the penalty, borrowing and selling. If all ethical reasoning were of this sort – an ethic of 'my station and its duty' – very little of it would be about distant hunger (Bradley, 1876; Hoffman, 1981; Walzer, 1981, 1983). For there is no shared institutional or ideological context which defines what the problems are or whose problems they are, let alone what remedies or solutions are acceptable.

If there can be ethical reasoning which reaches beyond local boundaries, it must have ways of identifying agents, problems, and principles of action which are not peculiar to local context. Philosophical writing in ethics has traditionally aspired to show how ethical reasoning could be prised away from local context. The very ambition to do so has also long been criticized. Ethical reasoning which abstracts wholly from local ethical codes and social structures must, it is feared, be inaccessible to actual agents. Since ethical reasoning about distant ills has no common social or ideological context, it cannot determine an agenda of problems, or allocate them to agents or propose remedies or solutions in terms that are accessible to whatever agents or agencies may have the power to change matters. Such reasoning might indeed be accessible to *idealized* agents on whom some ethical theory confers appropriate categories and reasoning capacities, but for actual agents and agencies it may be alien and inaccessible. If ethical reasoning is to cross ideological and social boundaries, it must be accessible not to idealized agents but to a variety of actual agents and agencies. Some consideration of the capacities of agents and agencies who can affect famines and endemic hunger is therefore fundamental in practical reasoning about these problems.

Recent work in applied ethics has said less about these problems than is needed. The central problem for *practical* reasoning is often taken to be that of finding principles of action that are both action-guiding and justifiable. Writing in ethics that relies on 'ideal' accounts of rational choosing treats the need for practical reasoning to be accessible to those who have to choose and to act as a minor and insignificant problem. Problems of communication and persuasion are not seen as serious ethical concerns, with the result that judgement may be 'abstracted from the context of the audience for which it is intended' (Beiner, 1983, p. 85). Even when it is acknowledged that 'ideal' rational choosing is impossible in contexts of action, this may be taken to mean only that applied ethical reasoning must lack the full precision and power of resolution of abstract theories of ethical reasoning (Simon, 1957; Hare, 1981). However, neither idealization nor imprecision guarantees accessibility for actual audiences. What is at stake is not whether ethical reasoning can guide action with ideal precision, but whether it can guide action at all.

3   Agents and Agencies

If ethical reasoning is to guide action in actual, particular cases, both the major and minor premises invoked must be *accessible* to those whose action or policies are to be guided by the reasoning. This is a more subtle and controversial requirement than it may at first seem, and leads to unwelcome difficulties.

Initial difficulties centre on the question: to whom can practical reasoning on matters that spread across national and ideological boundaries be addressed? Reasoning which is accessible must be conducted in terms of categories and concepts which are not only understood but taken to be appropriate by its presumed audience. It need not, and usually does not, provide reasons which are sufficient to determine action. Reasoning can be accessible even when it is not motivationally sufficient, but it must construe the problems faced in ways that strike its audience as relevant and must propose ethical standards, criteria and arguments which are accessible to them. If it relies on inaccessible starting points, ethical reasoning will seem to speak in alien and irrelevant categories or to rely on some mythical 'universal' mode of moral discourse. Yet how is a heterogeneous audience to be addressed without a universal mode of ethical discourse? How can the widely scattered and socially and ideologically divided individuals, institutions and collectivities who may affect the risk and course of world hunger and poverty be addressed in ways that are accessible to all, or even widely accessible?

A classical, eighteenth-century solution to this problem is to rely on modes of discourse which are thought to be accessible to 'rational beings as such' regardless of social or ideological formation. If every individual human being has access to certain common concepts and modes of thought, these can provide the desired universal vocabulary for practical reasoning. The way to transcend local and context-bound modes of ethical reasoning is to speak directly to individuals. Paradoxically, universal ethical reasoning can address only individuals.

If this is indeed the price of universally accessible ethical reasoning, it is a very high price. It would make ethics primarily a private matter, at best indirectly important in public affairs, and mainly relevant in thinking about personal dilemmas and relationships. Ethical reasoning would be inaccessible to powerful institutions and collectivities. It could not guide the action either of states, international bodies and transnational corporations, or of ethnic, national, religious and other social groups. None of these are ideal rational choosers. All are bound to the particular categories and concepts embodied in their constitution or tradition. They will find reasoning directed at ideal rational choosers inaccessible, and cannot be agents in the required sense. At best individualist reasoning can fix some boundary to institutional and collective action. It may, for example, insist that public action be limited by the prior ethical importance of spheres of individual action, or that public officials be required to 'keep their hands clean'. Much recent ethical writing, especially that centred on human rights, tries to work within these limitations. They are severe barriers for discussions of global problems.

Development studies may be filled with controversy over what the problems are and whose problems they are and how they ought to be tackled. However, there is no disagreement that ending hunger for all who now suffer or risk it needs major economic and political changes which cannot be produced by individual action alone. We may think, for example, that the roots of some famine, or of persistent poverty and hunger, lie in a system of land-tenure that leaves many without either title to food or access to work, or that it reflects the persistence of high fertility after dramatic rises in expectation of life, or that it is due to the exploitative practices of certain transnational corporations. There are deep differences between these diagnoses, but none of them identifies *individuals* who can reasonably be brought to task for their contribution or who can readily be required to reduce or avert the risk of famine and weight of destitution. In each case any individuals involved may have done no more than their positions seem to demand. Peasants and landlords, parents of large families and members of Third-World elites, transnational executives and super-power policy-makers may all protest that famines and hunger are not *their* doing or responsibility. They may neither intend to make or leave others hungry, nor foresee that their actions will contribute to hunger; and they may have good reasons for the actions or policies that they pursue. No doubt such claims are sometimes disingenuous: sometimes harms are intended or foreseen, and sometimes the good reasons claimed for an action or policy are insufficient, but often enough the claim that no individual is responsible seems plausible. If agency is seen as individual and connected to social role it may also seem that helping the hungry, though meritorious, is not obligatory, since obligations are fixed by the 'normal' ethics of locally accepted codes and standards.

A common response to such thoughts is to *avoid* the question of agency, and so avoid discussing *to whom* ethical reasoning should be accessible. This may be done by using ethical principles or theories which do not make explicit claims about agency. For example, consequentialist ethical reasoning aims to identify whatever action or policies – whether pursued by individuals, legislators, social groups, or nation states – is likely to maximize human happiness. In working this out, the varied capacities for ethical deliberation and for action of the presumed 'agents' may seem irrelevant; it is sufficient if the actions considered are 'available'. Yet what is *actually* available to individuals, collectivities and institutions will always reflect capacities for deliberation and action. Acts and policies are genuinely available, as opposed to logically possible, only if the agents or agencies who are to pursue them have appropriate cognitive capacities and powers of action. They must understand the categories employed and see them as relevant to the actual context, and have the power to take and to implement decisions. Taken in the abstract, consequentialist reasoning may not need an explicit conception of agency. However, if it is to guide deliberation in contexts of action, where it matters which acts and policies are really available, questions about agency have to be raised and settled, and the availability of modes of reasoning and lines of action to actual agents and agencies must be assured. Even individuals' capacities to understand and to act standardly depend on collective and institutional structures which provide education and socialization and define the powers and mandates of various collectivities and institutions and of social roles within them. Ethical reasoning cannot be shown accessible to institutions and collectivities just by *avoiding* explicit views of agency.

The need for an explicit account of agency cannot, however, be satisfied by returning to any idealized account of agency of the sorts discussed or assumed in individualist ethical reasoning. For reasoning which presupposes *idealized* capacities to reason and to act may often be as inaccessible to *actual* individuals as it is to collectivities and institutions. The individual agents whom ethical reasoning must reach are not *abstract* individuals in the sense of *idealized* individuals with comprehensive cognitive capacities and powers to act. Actual individuals have finite, socially and ideologically formed cognitive capacities, and powers of action that are limited and defined by social context. Although natural persons are very different from artificial persons, their capacities to understand and to act are also to a great extent artificial (O'Neill, 1984b). Ethical reasoning in which idealized capacities are assumed may then be *generally* inaccessible and so *generally* unsuitable to guide actual deliberation. An exclusively individualist picture of human agency is wholly inappropriate for deliberating about problems of famine and persistent hunger; it is avowedly inaccessible to collectivities and institutions, and often inaccessible to actual human individuals.

A more plausible approach to these problems might begin by discarding the assumption that agency is paradigmatically individual agency, let alone idealized individual agency. If famine and world hunger can be reduced and ended only with the action and collaboration of agents and agencies of many different sorts, any relevant practical reasoning must be accessible to institutions and collectivities and not just to individuals.

A first step towards an adequate account of agency is to acknowledge the agency of the great variety of institutions whose mandate requires them to work for famine relief and development. However, it would not be enough to see the agency of these institutions merely in terms of the categories and principles that constitute their charter and mandate. Many of those who work for such institutions, and others who criticize them, worry that their constitutions and working practices prevent them from achieving what their charters mandate. Aid agencies, both international and voluntary, get caught up in rivalries and mutual obstruction (McNeill, 1981; Shawcross, 1984); sometimes they fail to respond fast enough to dire emergencies (McNeill, 1981; Shepherd, 1975). The IMF is often criticized *within* development studies for following monetary policies which are against the interests of the poorest nations (Brandt, 1980, 1983). Development strategies, endorsed by the World Bank, by many Third-World governments and by transnational corporations, which have favoured investment in industrial capacity and in cash crops, rather than in subsistence agriculture, are now widely criticized (Brandt, 1980, 1983; Sen, 1981; Jackson, 1982; Dinham and Hines, 1983; Hartmann and Boyce, 1983; George, 1984; Hancock, 1985). These are not the cavils of a few eccentric critics. They are criticisms made by those with long and varied experience in problems of development, and on behalf of many of the most influential development institutions.

It follows that no adequate discussion of ethical reasoning about famine, poverty and hunger can take for granted *present* individuals and institutions, their ways of construing and allocating problems or their principles of practical reasoning. No account of agents and agencies can be taken for granted as the neutral presupposition of such ethical reasoning. Rather, a basic concern for such reasoning must be the *development of agents and agencies* whose capacities are adequate to the problems they are supposed to face (Brandt, 1980, 1983).

The configuration of agency can be changed in many ways. Both individuals and institutions can acquire new capacities to recognize and respond to different types of problems; and both can have their powers of action reduced or extended. However, transformations of existing agents and agencies must themselves be proposed in terms that are accessible to agents and agencies as they now are.

The picture of institutional and collective agency which such an account of ethical reasoning needs is not fully developed in this book. Broadly, it is that all actual agents and agencies (as opposed to the idealized rational agents of so much ethical and political theory) fall far short of 'perfect' rationality and of 'perfect' freedom. Both their cognitive abilities and their powers of action – and hence their autonomy – are limited and determinate. This is as true of actual human beings as it is of various institutions and collectivities. For ethical reasoning to be accessible to the individuals, institutions and collectivities to whom it is addressed they must have *some* capacities for guiding their action by deliberation, to which the proposed reasoning can be appropriately adjusted. They do not need ideal capacities. Many institutions and collectivities have this much; and actual human agents have no more. Accessible ethical reasoning has to address the actual and varied capacities for agency of different individuals, institutions and collectivities. Only if we had reasons to think that human agency is quite different from the agency of institutions and collectivities would individuals be the only audience for ethical reasoning.

The long traditions in ethics which hold that all agency is individual human agency are unconvincing in the light of the limited understanding and powers of action of actual human agents. We have, at our best, finite capacities to categorize, absorb and manipulate information; and equally at our best we have quite limited capacities to act in ways that will not sit well with our own inclinations, with others' preferences or with the institutional and social contexts within which we act. Often we are not at our best. If the partial capacities of institutions and collectivities were *general* barriers to their being agents, actual human individuals would seldom be agents either.

Institutions and collectivities too have limited capacities for agency. Although their typical limitations differ from those of human individuals, human agency is not in all ways more extensive than institutional agency. Individual memory and capacity to assimilate information may be more heterogeneous, but is often less accurate and less systematic than the corresponding capacities of government or other bureaucracies. Individuals' capacities to resist others' pressure and persuasion and caprice may also be less than the corresponding capacities of many institutions such as courts, bureaucracies or corporations. Individual capacities to form and articulate thoughts are seldom as versatile and complex as those which develop in collectivities that share tradition, conversation and debate.

Individuals' capacities to act are also often less than those of institutions and collectivities, although more versatile. There are indeed many acts which institutions and collectivities cannot do. Institutions cannot (literally) day-dream or give birth or climb mountains; no collectivity can become a hermit or first violinist. Equally, there are many acts which individuals can do only in institutionally or collectively structured contexts. No individual acting alone can marry or get divorced, promise or contract, form or dissolve a partnership, sell or buy a commodity, or negotiate or break a treaty. All of these actions must be mediated by institutions, and actions such as expressing public opinion or following traditional ways are impossible outside the context of a certain collectivity. Other actions are simply impossible for individuals, even in an appropriate social context. No individual can devalue a currency or irrigate a desert or have a debate on the best criteria for a soft loan policy. Individuals can only take a part in such activities in appropriate social contexts.

Although human individuals are unusually versatile agents, many of their actions are mediated by institutions and collectivities. There are no adequate grounds to insist that all ethical reasoning which takes the notion of agency seriously must be directed to individuals. Indeed an ethical theory which can address only beings with *unlimited, idealized* capacities to act would be equally useless for the deliberations of institutions and collectivities and for the deliberations of actual human individuals. Accessible ethical reasoning must take account of the *actual* capacities to understand and to act of the agents and agencies it addresses. Where these are inadequate to the tasks and obligations to which deliberation points, the transformation of individual, institutional and collective capacities for agency will be vital for other changes. Hence the present structure and limitations of the powers and capacities of many sorts of institution and collectivity provide no more *general* reason for thinking them incapable of development and of practical deliberation than do the corresponding limitations of present individual agents. We do not have any fixed account of agents and agencies which all reasoning about hunger and poverty can presuppose. On the contrary, transformations of the powers of agents and of agencies is itself likely to be central to any adequate development policy.

4   Established and Establishment Views

The enlarged picture of agency just sketched is needed for ethical deliberation which is accessible to a broad range of institutions and collectivities as well as to individual agents. It is an indispensable framework for practical deliberation which can be accessible to the varied agents and agencies who can reduce or exacerbate problems of poverty and hunger at a given time. However, it returns us to the problem that individualist theories of agency were supposed to solve. If different agents and agencies have different categories of thought – different conceptual frameworks – how can any mode of practical reasoning be universally, or even widely, accessible? Must not ethical deliberation, like all practical deliberation, be local and contextual, accessible to some audiences and alien to others? How can it assist widespread deliberation about global problems?

When individual agents and social agencies vary in their capacities it seems that accessible practical reasoning must use whatever categories are established in the modes of discourse of each agent or agency. While it need not provide motivationally sufficient reasons for action, it has to offer what they can understand as a reason for action. Only if it does so could it be counted as practical *reasoning* rather than, say, as an exercise of authority. This suggests that practical reasoning must be sectoral. Only arguments conducted in bureaucratic terms can reach bureaucracies; only arguments using standard capitalist economic categories can reach transnational corporations and their executives; only arguments in terms of national interest and standard political categories can reach governments and government agencies; only arguments using the categories of individualist self interest or conscience can reach individual agents. Reasoning which uses inappropriate categories will go past its presumed audience, be inaccessible, and so not be genuinely practical reasoning.

If we take so strong a view of what is needed for ethical reasoning to be accessible, all reasoning that is practical will be local and contextual, an ethic of my station and its duties, our agency and its mandate, our business and its priorities and responsibilities, and our nation and its interests. It would be as pointless to appeal to the conscience of an institution as it would be to hold up the ideals of liberal public life, such as impersonal fairness, in a traditional family context. Such a conception of what makes reasoning practical, in the sense of accessible, is essentially conservative; it cannot challenge or extend existing frameworks of thought, or current demarcations between the spheres of different institutions and practices, or put forward any universally accessible ethical claims. It is likely to be dominated by the categories of significant social agencies, and in public affairs today these are likely to be categories of nation states and their political institutions (see Walzer, 1983, p. 31):

> The idea of distributive justice presupposes a bounded world within which distributions take place: a group of people committed to dividing, exchanging, and sharing social goods, first of all among themselves. That world . . . is the political community, whose members distribute power to one another and avoid, if they possibly can, sharing it with anyone else. When we think about distributive justice, we think about independent cities or countries capable of arranging their own patterns of division and exchange, justly or unjustly.

This sectoral vision of practical reasoning would cripple ethical reasoning about problems, like those of famine and world hunger, whose remedy or alleviation needs coordinated action by many agents and agencies whose terms of reference and standard categories and discourse vary. If distributive justice is confined within national spheres, it cannot arbitrate between them, or between the interests of members of different spheres.

Another account of ethical reasoning is needed if it is to be accessible to diverse agents and agencies and to avoid these conservative implications. One approach might be to rely on terms and categories that are accessible to any agent or agency. Such reasoning would indeed be abstract, but need not take an idealized or merely individual view of cognitive capacities or powers of action. If the categories that are *actually* shared by all agents and agencies are few, however, this may leave us only with reasoning that fails to be practical in the other, action-guiding sense. The terms of discourse and modes of reasoning which are accessible to transnational executives, traditions of religious or tribal life and ideals of individual responsibility may have so little in common that the conceptions these agents and agencies share could support few action-guiding conclusions.

These considerations show some of the powerful reasons both for taking and for shunning abstract approaches to ethics. Abstraction from context became a marked feature of Western ethical thinking because it appeared to ground radical ethical demands for universal justice, and for discarding or overriding local and special ethical traditions which thwart such justice. This was all too often achieved by relying on patterns of reasoning which were accessible to hypothetical, idealized agents, but alien or inaccessible to many actual agents and agencies. Neither conservative appeals to established and establishment views nor liberal appeals to idealized views of universal rationality are enough to ground ethical deliberation which can appeal across boundaries and cultures.

A plausible account of accessible ethical reasoning would have to look in other directions. Reasoning may be accessible even if it does not use only our current ethical vocabulary, provided that the categories it uses are ones that we could come not merely to understand, but to see as salient and important. Accessible ethical reasoning may do no more than meet us half way. Reasoning which assumes a *total* transformation of the terms and categories of the agents or agencies it addresses will be inaccessible. Such transformations may at best be the products rather than the premises of accessible practical reasoning. Accessible ethical reasoning must be connected to what MacIntyre (1981, p. 205) has called the 'moral starting point' of those to whom it is addressed; but it may also transform both the principles and the perceptions of particular situations which constitute that starting point.

If we were able to follow only one ethical idiom, as relativists sometimes suggest, we could not hope for gradual or reasoned transitions from one moral outlook to another, but at best for 'conversions', in which a new way of looking at things is accepted as a whole. Our actual situation is more flexible. Nothing is more central to human reasoning than shifting between different possible descriptions of situations. We can understand and follow varied idioms, and may find that some are inappropriate to a certain domain of life, or blind to significant features and hypersensitive to others. New categories and idioms become accessible as their point is increasingly appreciated and evidenced. Relativist worries and claims of conceptual incommensurability between alien or rival ethical outlooks are understandably frequent during decades of halting passage from ethnocentric to wider perspectives, but even our daily experience of 'normal' practical reasoning gives the lie to the more extreme claims of relativists (see Gellner, 1983, p. 120):

The incommensurability thesis owes something of its plausibility to a tendency to take too seriously the self-absolutizing, critic-anathematizing faiths of late agrarian societies, which indeed are generally so constructed as to be logically invulnerable from outside and perpetually self-confirming from inside. Despite these notorious traits . . . the adherents of these faiths have known how to transcend their own much advertised blinkers. They are and were conceptually bilingual, and know how to switch from commensurate to incommensurate idioms with ease and alacrity.

So long as actual agents and agencies are 'multilingual', reasoned transformations of ethical starting points are possible.

5 Ethics and Ideology

Accessible practical reasoning often has to work by means of transformations of consciousness and ideology.[1] It does not have to stick to established terms of discourse but may aim to revise them. The terms of discourse of market economies, of the labour movement and of nationalism itself were once inaccessible – and perhaps incomprehensible. Where they gained currency new ethical problems could be discerned, and old ones mattered less. The boundaries between the 'spheres' of different agents and agencies, and allocations of problems to them, changed. Certain lines of action appeared suspect which had formerly been standard practice, and others became standard practice which had formerly been (perhaps literally) unthinkable. This is possible only because established categories and conceptual frameworks are in various ways 'porous'. If we were indeed dealing with idealized rational beings or rational economic men, or ideal typical Weberian bureaucracies and monolithic states, such transformation might be impossible – but the modes of discourse of actual agents and agencies are not closed. The imperviousness of distinct ideologies which would leave us with ethical, and indeed conceptual, relativism is an illusion produced by idealizing tendencies in ethics and in social science.

If ethical reasoning is accessible to agents and agencies that can affect the risk of famine and persistence of hunger and poverty, it must latch on to the categories and modes of discourse with which those agents and agencies are at home. It must connect both with the *principles* (including ethical principles) and with the *perceptions* of those whom it addresses. The categories used in ethical reasoning cannot then be *wholly* alien to the actual agents and agencies whose action is needed.

Yet these categories and modes of discourse cannot constitute the boundaries of ethical concern and reasoning. Some of them may be selfish, corrupt or blind. For example, the categories and rhetoric of nationalist movements often exclude or minimize concern for foreigners. The economic and financial categories which are the standard discourse in banking and in commodity markets may seem blind to the problems which high interest rates or volatile commodity prices create for the poor in fragile economies. The standard categories of daily discussion and acceptable action in many traditions may reflect a local outlook or ideology which extends concern to few beyond immediate kin and neighbours. Even when the fundamental principles to which appeal is made in some outlook or ideology *might* have implications for action affecting famine and hunger, locally established or preferred descriptions of actual situations may blunt or diffuse those implications.

Two steps are needed to prevent practical reasoning from becoming hostage to established and establishment views of how situations should be construed and problems remedied. First, plausible ethical *principles* must be identified and shown to be both able to guide action and accessible to the relevant audiences, and yet more than projections of locally established categories and discourse. Secondly, the *particular descriptions and appraisals of actual situations* invoked – the minor premises of ethical reasoning – must also be shown accessible to whatever audiences the reasoning addresses, and yet more than the preferred perspectives of local outlook. It can be particularly hard to prise perceptions away from whatever categories and discourse are locally established, especially in reasoning which is addressed to institutions and their officers.

Those who have to balance the books and keep or enforce the law, or pursue company policy or the national interest, may claim that they *cannot* construe situations in terms other than those of practices accepted in these institutions, nor act in ways which might be thought ethically required (in terms of one or another underlying principle) except where such action coincides or at least is consistent with the directives of the codes to which they are bound. The impotence individuals and collectivities may experience in the face of great and distant evils is often matched by the sense of impotence of officials and executives, who may express their (perhaps genuine) personal sympathy for those whom they do not help, and protest (possibly resent and regret) their inability to do what falls outside their institutional mandate.

A common response to these constraints has been to emphasize individual responsibility for joining or holding office in certain types of collectivity or institution. The approach gained prominence from its application to Nazi crimes. Individual members of the SS and of other Nazi organizations were judged responsible for their membership in institutions with certain underlying, criminal aims and for acts which they ordered or committed in furtherance of these aims. At Nuremberg the plea of obedience to superior orders was rejected, although it counted in mitigation (French, 1972, pp. 177–204; Walzer, 1977).

Enforcement of standards of individual responsibility is a weak constraint on the harms and wrongs done by institutions and collectivities. Yet if only human individuals are seen as agents, there is no other way in which to deal retrospectively with such harms and wrongs. However, this approach could not easily be used to curb or alter the action of collectivities or institutions which may harm or wrong the distant hungry or poor. The Nuremberg approach worked very selectively to punish Nazi criminals, in spite of the Nazi penchant for keeping records which documented who had ordered whom to do what. It also drew on a long tradition of internationally accepted ethical and legal standards. It added to the traditional categories of war crimes and crimes against peace (both of them long familiar in just war theory and in international conventions) the cognate category of crimes against humanity. There is no analogous nucleus of accepted standards of global distributive justice in terms of which the conduct of individuals who act for institutions which contribute to or exacerbate dire poverty could be judged. That, after all, is the underlying problem of which hunger and destitution are livid evidence. Its solution can hardly be assumed in this discussion.

In any case, retrospective judgements of responsibility, especially of individual responsibility, open a weak and indirect route to changing the action of powerful institutions and collectivities. What is to the point is to change the normal activities and boundaries of certain institutions and collectivities. These can be changed in fundamental ways only by altering established frames of reference for many agents and agencies. Such transformations can work through various channels. Some might use existing institutional structures to modify or reform or restrain the working of institutions, or to adjust the boundaries between them. Others might depend upon education or publicity – or perhaps propaganda – that alters the definition and agenda of certain institutions, or the horizons and boundaries of certain collectivities. At its most comprehensive such activities may transform the relationship between different institutions and collectivities and their relative importance, and may dissolve some and found others.

All activity which aims to transform and redraw the boundaries and powers of established institutions and practices is in a fundamental way political. Much political activity accepts the institutional and ideological context of its time and place. It is the politics of our nation and its interests, our party and its policies. Such 'normal' politics is the art of the *immediately* possible. Political activity within established structures may exacerbate rather than alleviate global hunger and poverty; their remedy may demand structural changes which need more than 'normal' politics.[2] The political activity that is ethically important would offer some critical appraisal of existing political structures and moves towards changing them. Practical reasoning which has this aim can be thought of as equally ethical and political. It is fundamentally ethical because it does not assume that existing categories and boundaries define either problems or solutions: it is fundamentally political because it does not assume that actual agents and agencies can be reached except by reasoning which relies at least in part on their present categories and boundaries. Activity that challenges and redefines established categories and practices of social life and the boundaries between different agencies and domains of life provides a framework for the deliberations of 'normal' politics and of 'normal' ethics. If 'applied' ethics and 'uplifted' politics do converge it will be because a context that is coherent for both has been established.

The task of establishing social structures and ways of thought that meet standards of critical appraisal may seem hopeless unless we accept that there are universally accessible standards of rationality which are sufficiently powerful to generate ethical standards.

However, if there is no Archimedean point from which all social and ideological structures can be assessed, must not all social and ideological structures, and so all 'normal' ethics and politics, be the handmaiden of established social structures and of dominant ideologies? Is not the image of a neutral standpoint for comprehensive critical judgement as much a fantasy as Plato's suggestion that the ideal city may be constructed by taking a new and unformed generation of children as its citizens? All thought and action of actual individuals, collectivities and institutions must, after all, bear the hall-mark of their settings.

However, those who hold that social and ideological structures not only provide a framework for 'normal' ethical and political reasoning, but are themselves impervious to all such reasoning, assume more than the lack of a neutral, transcendent standpoint. They assume also the mutual exclusiveness and imperviousness of alternative understandings of any situation, their resulting radical conceptual (and so ethical) incommensurability, and the mutual isolation of differing agents and agencies. Nevertheless, established or dominant ways of perceiving or construing the world are seldom the only ones accessible to those who hold or prefer them at a given time. Linguistic and conceptual structures are more or less indeterminate, and those who hold them can grasp other ways of perceiving the world and other principles of action. Provided that some variety of understanding is possible, there is enough to begin a process of critical appraisal of established modes of understanding. However, the direction of critical practical reasoning will not be *de haut en bas*; it will not be an 'external' assessment of all possible structures or viewpoints from the perspective of one transcendent viewpoint. It may be no more than the mutual criticism of standpoints which are grasped by a single agent or agency, whose outlook and activity struggles to do justice to both.

Agents and agencies with differing outlooks or ideologies need not be mutually insulated and isolated. Our varied success (and no doubt frequent failures) in understanding those with whom we disagree, even disagree radically, shows that radical conceptual incommensurability is a problem that arises in abstract thought, but seldom in human experience. Our cognitive capacities are more varied, more versatile, more porous and open to other ways of construing the world and its problems than those who fear radical conceptual isolation allow.

Nor is it only the categorial framework of individual agents which has an open and porous character. Collectivities can also acquire new ways of seeing the world. The widespread transformation of attitudes towards slavery and racism and democracy during the last century, and the incomplete changes in perception of ethnocentrism and gender chauvinism in our own, are clear examples of changes which go far beyond individual changes of view. Institutions too can be more open to conceptual innovation and transformation than abstract discussions may suggest. 'Ideal-typical' bureaucracies or corporations may have a fixed and limited conceptual repertoire, so can respond only to a narrow range of modes of practical reasoning and are blind to problems described in ways that do not match their competence. If actual institutions were of this sort it would be pointless, indeed sentimental, to address ethical reasoning that was not confined to their own idiom to them. Most actual institutions are less tautly structured than the idealized theoretical structures of social science. Any major restructuring of an institution may be in part a transformation of its cognitive and decision-making capacities and powers of action which allows for new construals of some domain of problems and of the range of reasons to which the institution is responsive and changes in the range of actions and policies which fall within its ambit.

6   Algorithms and Principles

In reasoning for changes in the moral starting points of various individuals, collectivities and institutions it is not enough to achieve transformations in their perception of certain domains of problems. Heightened awareness alone provides no reasons for action. Reasoning which is fully practical must also be able to guide action. The underlying, major premises or principles of practical reasoning must combine with appropriate minor premises or descriptions of situations to provide reasons for some rather than other policies or actions to be pursued or avoided by particular agents and agencies. Reasoning which is not in any way *action-guiding* just is not practical reasoning. It provides no principles by which actual deliberation can lead to judgements about actions or policies.

Principles and theories may be able to guide action, even if they are abstract, provided that they do not depend on inaccurate idealizations, but there is considerable disagreement over the degree of guidance needed. Some ethical theories propose as the major premises for ethical reasoning principles that could (given appropriate minor premises and procedures of deliberation) guide action with great precision. For example, some sorts of consequentialist reasoning, such as utilitarianism, can in theory rank available actions in order of merit, so showing which act or policy is best, which next best, and so on. In practice, many consequentialists hold, complete and precise information is not usually available. Yet the theory offers an ambitious practical *algorithm* as the major premise for guiding action among available alternatives.

Principles can, however, guide action without providing any practical algorithm. Some ethical theories merely propose a test for detecting some categories of actions and policies. A theory that offers a decision procedure for obligatoriness can show whatever fails the test forbidden, and whatever is required to avoid such failure obligatory. Ethical theories which provide a decision procedure for obligations, or for some other important ethical feature, do not aim to rank all actions or policies, or to single out one as the best available. Here too the reasoning may be more or less precise; but even if great precision were possible such theories could not guide action as firmly or fully as consequentialist reasoning purports to. They would rule out certain acts (or omissions) or policies as ethically unacceptable, and rule in others as ethically required. For many contexts such decision procedures may be sufficiently action-guiding.

Still other ethical theories propose principles that could guide action only indirectly, by pointing to or requiring some state of character or virtue or some type of life. A life informed by courage or compassion can indeed guide action, for there are some things that those with courage or compassion cannot do, and perhaps others that they must, in given circumstances, do or pursue. Here action is guided indirectly. Such theories may be important in moral education, since we can rarely tell just which problems will arise for anyone throughout a lifetime, so may not be able to propose informative principles for guiding action. In contexts of action, however, theories of virtue or of the good life may still not be enough to guide action. Action-guiding theories have to provide both principles and on account of deliberation by which those with courage or compassion can work out what these virtues demand in particular situations. A large element of moral education must be the development of powers of judgement and deliberation. Ethical reasoning which centres on notions of character or virtue is not *by itself* sufficiently articulated to resolve action-hindering disagreement about matters like famine and world hunger. Such theories will therefore not be further discussed in this book.

7   Agency, Perceptions and Principles

This chapter has argued for three standards to which ethical reasoning, at least about problems of the public domain, should aspire. First, it should be based on an accurate, nonidealized account of agency, which allows for the agency of institutions and collectivities as well as the agency of individuals. Secondly, it should employ ethical and other categories which are or can be made accessible to the agents and agencies whose action is required, without being coopted by whatever ethical outlook is already established. Thirdly, it should rely on ethical principles which have considerable – not necessarily algorithmic – power to resolve dilemmas.

One implication of these standards is that ideology and received views are relevant to ethical deliberation. They provide the 'moral starting points' from which we must work. However, if the view offered here of the open character not only of individual outlook but of the established views and categories of collectivities and institutions is correct, we can move beyond starting points. One reasonable test of the adequacy of a body of ethical reasoning is its ability to reach those with diverse starting points and provide accessible reasons for changing these. In the following chapters three types of ethical theory will be considered from this viewpoint. Chapters 4 and 5 will consider consequentialist forms of reasoning; Chapter 6 will discuss reasoning which is based on claims about human rights; and Chapters 7 and 8 will turn to reasoning which makes the notions of obligation and need central. If any of these types of ethical theory is to be helpful in thinking about the incidence of famine and the persistence and increase in hunger, it must not only put forward principles which can be vindicated to those with varied moral starting points, but must incorporate modes of reasoning which assist moves beyond initial appraisals of the problems faced.

A short work dealing with a nexus of complex, controversial and often ill-understood problems cannot set out or defend a generally adequate and accessible account even of the more important minor premises relevant to the full range of problems of world hunger. Suggestions about the origin and remedy of famine can be no more than tentative and subject to revision and rejection. This difficulty may be less profound than it initially seems, for two reasons. First, actual deliberation is always undertaken by particular agents and agencies in particular contexts. *No* account of ethical reasoning could incorporate the whole gamut of minor premises that might be relevant to every occasion. At best it must use what are taken to be typical accounts of problems and situations and treat these as illustrative of a broader range of arguments that may be pertinent in actual contexts. Secondly, even if these typical accounts are later seen as inadequate or defective, they are nevertheless what we have to begin from. They are what is now accessible from a certain actual context. We cannot await a comprehensive account of the nature and remedy of world hunger – for if we do nothing in the meantime we may excerbate the problems rather than leave them untouched. The accounts and judgements on which we rely may be flawed; but if we do not rely on them at all the possibility of reasoning about hunger is postponed indefinitely.

The first concern of this book is therefore not to reach definitive minor premises for describing some hunger problems, but to find appropriate major premises. *If* these can be found and defended they may also help us discern appropriate minor premises. The search for appropriate major premises is not simply a matter of selecting among the more promising or reputable ethical theories, for many of these theories have features which, at first glance, make them unsuitable for dealing with problems which are neither produced nor remediable by individual action. It is in the first place a search for ways of deliberating that meet the standards outlined here, can be of use for institutions and collectivities as well as individuals, yet can resist cooption by locally established modes of ethical discourse and criticize ways in which these constrain both perceptions and prescriptions for action. If we find any ethical theory which has these capacities, we may still be far from finding action-guiding and accessible solutions to the many problems of world hunger and poverty, and from being able to convince the various agents and agencies who could make a difference, but we may have reached a position from which moves towards such solutions are not in principle inaccessible.

Notes

1 'Ideology' is used here, and will be used, in a merely descriptive sense, to refer to the concepts and beliefs, as well as the debates and disagreements, that link some human group. There is no suggestion that ideologies are invariably false, or distorting, nor that they are beyond criticism; nor is any claim about the origins, content or scope of any or all ideologies implied (cf. Geuss, 1981, ch. 1).

2 Why the persistent scare quotes on 'normal'? As a reminder that such reasoning need not be standard or typical, but rather must depend on some framework of norms; also to avert analogies with the Kuhnian contrast between normal and revolutionary science. Political and ethical activity which contrasts with 'normal' ethics and politics need not be revolutionary in the standard political sense.

4

Reasoning about Results

What did utilitarianism have going for it? A lot of things undoubtedly: its seeming compatibility with scientific thought; its this-worldly humanist focus, its concern with suffering. But one of the powerful background factors behind much of this appeal was *epistemological*. A utilitarian ethic seemed to be able to fit the canons of rational validation as these were understood in the intellectual culture nourished by the epistemological revolution of the seventeenth century. . . .

In the utilitarian perspective, one validated an ethical position by hard evidence. You count the consequences for human happiness of one or another course, and you go with the highest total. . . . One could abandon all the metaphysical and theological factors – commands of God, natural rights, virtues – which made ethical questions scientifically undecidable. Bluntly, we could calculate. (Taylor, 1982, p. 129)

Utilitarianism is better at providing one with a good conscience than a good compass. (Hoffman, 1981, p. 43)

1 Taking Results Seriously

Consequentialist patterns of ethical reasoning offer evident advantages for discussing both famine and persistent poverty and hunger. Since the results of whatever is done – or not done – are evidently grave here, reasoning which centres on results seems to the point. Where actions or policies may affect not only the character and quality of many lives but their very possibility, results cannot be neglected. When the dangers are great we may see no point in good intentions, in good character or even in right action unless they are accompanied, perhaps even defined, by good results.

A second reason for thinking consequential reasoning particularly promising for deliberation about problems of famine and hunger is that it is not tied to a stringent or narrow account of agency.[1] All results, whether produced by individual, institutional or by collective action, are open to consequential assessment; and consequential reasons for or against certain sorts of action are often accessible to institutions and collectivities as well as to individuals. Natural events are the only producers of results that cannot be directly addressed by consequential practical reasoning: we can be pretty sure that the weather system is deaf to reasons of all sorts. However, natural events and their results are taken into account in consequential reasoning, since all reckoning of consequences draws on knowledge of natural regularities.

A third reason for thinking consequential reasoning a promising departure point is that it is well entrenched both in the daily life and practice and in the more explicit decision-making procedures of many agents and agencies. Countless individual decisions are reached in part by considering which available action appears to lead to better results, or how results which are seen as good might be produced. The social and economic activities of daily life are often guided by such thinking. Farmers and consumers, shopkeepers and employees, managers and economic planners are all familiar with consequentialist patterns of thought, which are in part constitutive of many social practices. In some institutions consequential reasoning is mandated, as when cost–benefit studies must be used to choose between alternative policies. We can therefore be sure that aspects of consequentialist deliberating are accessible for many individual agents and social agencies.

Consequential practical deliberation, it seems, should be able to pick out actions and policies likely to reduce hunger and poverty and then recommend them in terms that are accessible to agents and agencies whose capacities and powers enable them to make changes. So it is not surprising that many discussions of ethical problems of famine and development have been broadly consequentialist. Yet closer consideration of such discussions shows that they often depend on ethical considerations which are not at home within consequentialist thinking and that there are disconcerting disagreements between consequentialist writers on famine, hunger and poverty.

2   Consequentialist Reasoning in the Abstract

The lynchpin of consequentialist deliberation is the simple thought that action is right if it leads to good results. This abstract starting point must be extended in several ways to develop a decision procedure for action. Four sorts of addition, at least, are indispensable.

First it is essential to provide some account of what makes results good. Attempts to provide an objective account of the good begin with Plato's *Republic*. These accounts have so far been dogged by epistemological opacity. In addition, many modern attempts to work out an objective account of the good, from G. E. Moore's *Principia Ethica* onwards, have had rather little to say about the ethical problems of the public domain. These theories, as so far developed, are therefore not likely to help us think about the ethical problems of famine, hunger and poverty.

The vast majority of modern consequentialist thinkers have preferred an empirical, indeed subjective, account of what makes results good. Most adopt one or another form of utilitarianism, but differ in their claims about just what it is that makes results good. The more traditional and robust claim with Bentham that 'utility' is whatever produces 'pleasure and the absence of pain' and makes results good, and that pleasures and pains can be aggregated with mathematical precision. Not all share Bentham's cheerful conviction (see Bentham, 1789, Vol. I, pp. 1–2) that we do not need to be too careful in determining what it is that makes results good since

> By utility is meant that property in any object, whereby it tends to produce benefit, advantage, pleasure, good or happiness (all this comes to the same thing).

Nor do all share his confidence that we can devise a *felicific calculus* for computing the expected utility of any available action. Utilitarians since John Stuart Mill have often doubted that pleasures were sufficiently homogeneous to be aggregated or measured with any precision. A great deal of utilitarian effort has gone into the task of finding an account of good results which is *precise* enough for comparing the merits of different results, yet *distant* enough from the most nearly measurable sensory pleasures to be a plausible measure of value. In recent and sophisticated formulations, the subjective starting point is often well-hidden and many of its less appealing implications are deflected; yet it remains a persistent source of difficulties (cf. Sen, 1977; Scheffler, 1982; Schick, 1982; Taylor, 1982).

The second essential component of any utilitarian pattern of practical reasoning is to have some method by which to identify which actions are available. In the abstract this is easy enough: we need only posit that some list of actions includes all that are available and give each an identifying label. However, as we shall see, this aspect of utilitarian reasoning can lead to trouble in actual contexts of deliberation and action.

The third essential component for any utilitarian pattern of reasoning is a sufficient range of causal knowledge for the probable results of available courses of action (under plausible assumptions about other factors, including the capacities of the relevant agents and agencies) to be known with reasonable accuracy. Without this knowledge, no link between available actions and good or bad results can be forged.

The fourth and last essential element of consequential reasoning is a clear account of the relationship between claims about what is good and claims about what is right. The formulation that actions that lead to good results are right is, by itself, too vague to guide action, since there may be many ways in which to produce good results. Classical utilitarians take the view that whichever action produces the best results is not merely *a* right action (i.e. permissible), but *the* right action (i.e. obligatory). Such *maximizing* principles for ranking available actions are *algorithmic*; they can (in conjunction with the first three requirements) determine which available action is morally required in any given situation. Various recent utilitarians reject maximizing principles of right action in favour of ranking principles which take account of the *distribution* of good results, so reduce the well-known insensitivity of utilitarian thought to questions of distribution. Others propose ranking principles which take account of some limits of agents' cognitive or other capacities, or emphasize the minimizing of harm rather than the maximizing of benefit.[2] However, any utilitarian – indeed any consequentialist – thinking needs *some* ranking principle which connects its concepts of the good and the right.

These four essential features make consequentialist reasoning extremely powerful, at least in the abstract. They constitute an algorithmic pattern of deliberation that can begin with consideration either of results or of action. If some result is known to be optimal (in terms of the preferred ranking procedure), causal knowledge can be used to pick out the act or policy that would best produce that result, so be obligatory. If the range of available actions and policies is known, causal knowledge can be used to predict their likely outcomes, so to judge which has the optimal results and is obligatory.

3   Consequentialist Discussions of Famine and Hunger

We might expect so powerful a pattern of deliberation to yield strong conclusions when applied to problems of famine and hunger, where many actions and policies seriously affect prospects for human happiness. Strong claims have indeed been made in various consequentialist writings on hunger and development, but some of these claims are wholly incompatible with others. On the surface it is puzzling that a pattern of thought which is close to algorithmic should lead to wildly diverse conclusions. A brief look at some of the disagreements shows that they are neither trivial nor easily dispelled.

One influential consequentialist writer on problems of famine and hunger is Peter Singer. His initial discussion of the topic in 'Famine, Affluence and Morality', first published in 1972 (p. 24), and extended and broadened in *Practical Ethics* (1979), uses an impeccably consequentialist starting point:

> if it is in our power to prevent something bad from happening, without thereby sacrificing anything of comparable moral importance, we ought morally to do it.

Since sacrifice of luxuries and even comforts typically harms human happiness far less than doing without necessities, Singer concludes that the rich, and even the moderately well-off, ought to give their surplus to the poor until they have so reduced their standard of living that further giving would indeed sacrifice 'something of comparable moral importance'. Doing without a car will produce no more than inconvenience; but the money it saves, suitably transferred, can end much acute hunger or illness. Consequentialist reasoning coupled with marginalist considerations show that the (relatively) rich ought to give to the poor until doing so is producing more harm than benefit.

Singer's position and others like it are sometimes criticized because they demand heroic self-sacrifice. Net benefit is likely to rise until a very high proportion of income has been transferred to the poor. For consequentialists 'only the best will do'; by making a life of relentless optimizing obligatory they leave no room for good but suboptimal action (cf. Kagan, 1984). They are likely to suffer an 'overload of obligations'. Nonconsequentialists are likely to worry about this since it appears to leave no room for things that many of them value, such as nonpaternalism, the preservation of a sphere of what Mill called 'self-regarding actions' and a corollary respect for personal projects and (some) rights (Fishkin, 1982, pp. 70–79, 145–149).

Both Singer's account of the implications of consequentialism and Fishkin's criticism of them appear sharper because they take it that consequential reasoning mainly addresses individuals. Consequentialist deliberation which was aimed primarily at social institutions and practices might stress individual giving and heroic effort less and its calculations of net benefit would surely take into account the social isolation that heroic consequentialists inflict on themselves and their families in current social conditions, while allowing that under other social conditions much larger transfers might harm the rich or moderately well-off less.

Therefore, it seems that Singer is mistaken when he claims in his more recent work (Singer, 1979, pp. 168–169) that his starting point should be acceptable to non consequentialists, since it says nothing about helping the poor or hungry by sacrificing whatever they may think 'of comparable moral importance'. It does indeed *say* nothing about such sacrifices – but so long as there is no upper bound on the obligations of beneficence, there will be no scope for indifferent or self-regarding action and no obligation to respect liberties. However, a variant consequentialism might place an upper limit on heroic giving, or set aside the problem as arising only in a misleadingly individualist version of consequentialism. The important point in Singer's position (1979, p. 169) is not that it leaves too little room for anything but beneficence, but that it makes it entirely clear that beneficence is a matter of obligation:

Helping is not, as conventionally thought, a charitable act which it is praiseworthy to do, but not wrong to omit; it is something that everyone ought to do.

This is the central substantive ethical claim for any consequentialist. All obligations are fundamentally required because they contribute to human happiness or benefit, and right action is in the first place helpful or beneficent action. Obligations of justice are not separate from, let alone more fundamental than, obligations of beneficence. The most necessary sorts of help to others can indeed be *called* duties of justice rather than of charity; but they are nonetheless grounded in a general duty of beneficence (J. S. Mill, 1861, ch. 5).

This much is common ground among consequentialists. Yet as we try to determine the more specific implications of the position, we find many disagreements. In his earlier article, Singer argued for generous private giving. However, other consequentialists argued that gifts and aid, while no doubt generously intended, were actually wrong on consequentialist grounds, since they produce greater misery in the long run than a policy of *laissez faire* (Hardin, 1974; references in Lucas and Ogletree, 1976).

The nub of Hardin's argument is that help, especially in the form of food aid, encourages the poor to have more children, so leads to increases of population, with the long-term result that the numbers of the destitute increase to a point at which no help or aid can prevent savage and widespread famine. Hardin likens the world's predicament to a shipwreck. Some of us – the rich – have found seats in lifeboats; others – the poor – are swimming desperately in the water. If those in the lifeboats rescue the drowning they will make the boats unseaworthy, and in the long run more will drown. By contrast, Hardin (1974, p. 17) claims:

If poor countries received no food aid from outside, the rate of their growth would be periodically checked by crop failures and famines. But if they can always draw on a world food bank in time of need, their population can continue to grow unchecked, and so will their 'need' for aid. In the short run a world food bank may diminish that need, but in the long run it actually increases that need without limit.

Hardin's neo-Malthusian vision has been repeatedly challenged. His shipwreck analogy obscures many differences. When there are not enough seats in lifeboats, further rescues evidently risk lives. There is no evidence that the world is now suffering from over-all food shortage; indeed, there is often ample food close to acute famines (Shepherd, 1975; Sen, 1981). There is no conclusive evidence that the rate of population growth in poor countries will not fall, just as it has fallen in the formerly poor countries which make up the now-developed world (Boserup, 1981; *People*, 1984).

However, in his more recent writing Singer moves closer to some of Hardin's conclusions. He maintains that utilitarian reasoning cannot endorse the certain evil of refusing aid to those in greatest need, but argues for refusing aid to countries that do not slow their population growth, and for concentrating aid where it will be more effective (Singer, 1979, pp. 178–179). This he admits 'could be very harsh on the poor citizens of those countries', but is still required of consequentialists if they discover that refusing such aid will be most likely to maximize happiness.

It would be misleading to think of this amendment to Singer's position as a complete convergence of his position with Hardin's. Hardin's entire position rejects the use of aid, supposedly for the sake of the best available long term; Singer wants the allocation of aid to be as effective as possible. His more recent writings advocate both government and private aid, and the use of political leverage to encourage reforms in land-tenure arrangements or international trade policies, or in any other institution or practice that may be contributing to the risk of hunger. Singer still rejects Hardin's conclusions not because they cannot be reached by a consequentialist route, but because Hardin's claims about the demographic results of aid rely on causal generalizations that Singer thinks mistaken, or at least not proven. There can be no warrant in consequentialist thinking for adopting emergency measures, which are certain to bring added misery to many, if we are neither sure that there is that sort of emergency nor that supposedly 'tough' measures will end it.

More recently, another group of controversies has mushroomed on the same consequentialist turf. These concern the sorts of aid policies that should be pursued. While Singer argued for a broad spectrum of policies, ranging from the provision of

food and development aid, and from private forms of charity to
various sorts of government programmes, others think some
sorts of aid are unhelpful, or even dangerous to the poor. The
criticisms are numerous and diverse; many of them come from
those who have worked with or for aid and development agencies,
both voluntary and governmental (McNeill, 1981; Jackson, 1982;
Dinham and Hines, 1983).

Bilateral aid policies have been criticized because they offer too
much opportunity for 'donor' countries to pursue their national
or economic interests, or those of certain corporations, at the
expense of the needs of underdeveloped areas (Wallerstein, 1980;
McNeill, 1981; Kitching, 1982; IGBA, 1983). 'Aid' that is con-
ditional on importing the products of certain companies or on
certain political concessions or privileged trade arrangements
may cost an underdeveloped country, or some of its people, more
than the benefits it brings. Development loans that must be paid
for at very high interest rates may damage rather than foster
economic progress.

Multilateral as well as bilateral aid policies have been criticized
for concentrating too much on capital-intensive and high-
technology projects, which may benefit a developed enclave but
not the poor, whose already meagre opportunities for employment they may reduce (McNeill, 1981; Sen, 1981; Dinham and
Hines, 1983; Hartmann and Boyce, 1983). In some cases the
regulations and safeguards imposed on aid, often to ensure
accountability, efficiency and lack of corruption, are so complex
and hard to meet that there appears from the perspective of
'donor' agencies to be a dearth of 'fundable' projects, and rival
agencies may end up competing for the 'good' projects (Brandt,
1980, 1983; McNeill, 1981). The supposedly beneficent results of
insisting on tight control of aid funds and projects by donor
agencies has now been queried (McNeill, 1981, p. 103):

Aid donors are faced by two alternatives. One is to go
further along the road of controls: to devise more sophisticated techniques of planning, appraisal and implementation
and become still more involved in the decision making
processes of the recipient countries, while preserving the
myth that they merely provide what is requested of them.
The second is to allow recipients more control, to make aid

more automatic, and to concede at least some power over the purse strings.

Even food aid, which seems so clear a benefit to those who are actually hungry, has been criticized. Government-to-government food aid gives Third-World governments (who sell the food they are given to raise revenue) excessive control and damages indigenous agricultural systems by destroying the market for locally grown cereals. Even 'project' food aid, which aims to give food directly to those whose need is most severe often fails to do so, and again actually harms the poorest indirectly by damaging local agriculture (Jackson, 1982). Many forms of food aid benefit the productive farmers of the developed world, who are able to sell more of their surplus at high prices subsidized by their own taxpayers; but it is not clear that it always benefits those to whom the food is given. As more and more nations, especially in Africa, become less and less food self-sufficient (Dinham and Hines, 1983), the simple policy of getting food to the hungry to which consequentialist reasoning seemed so obviously to point, begins to seem suspect. Tony Jackson (1982, p. 93) writes of various forms of damaging food aid:

It has been assumed up to now that food aid is needed because there is a shortage of food in the Third World. The Third World is thus seen as a vast refugee camp with hungry people lining up for food from the global food aid soup kitchen. This view is false. Some disasters aside (and these are important areas for food aid), the basic problem is not one of food, but poverty. Free handouts of food do not address this problem, they aggravate it.

Jackson has not, of course, adopted Hardin's position. He is suggesting that food aid is the wrong response to persistent hunger and poverty, and may even harm those whom it is meant to benefit, if too little account is taken of the longer-term economic effects of destroying farmers' livelihood by supplying free or subsidized food. In seeing the Third World as 'a vast refugee camp', we would be misled by the publicity and rhetoric used by many development agencies and concerned individuals and forget that the vast majority of the desperately poor are not starving refugees or victims of sudden catastrophe. They are leading their ordinary lives in unproductive and fragile economic systems, which are easily harmed by competition and exploitation from more productive economies (Franke and Chasin, 1979; Dinham and Hines, 1983; George, 1984). Yet this is not a startling new discovery. Anyone who wanted to discover the impact of a 'cheap food' policy on rural prosperity could have thought about the impact on British agriculture of the repeal of the Corn Laws in 1846.

The consequentialist disagreements sketched so far all presuppose that the underlying context in which policies and decisions that affect 'aid' and trade are made is the existing international economic order. They assume that the institutions which channel 'aid' and loans from developed to underdeveloped regions are dominated by the developed nations and responsive to financial criteria. Far wider areas of disagreement emerge if this context is not taken for granted. If aid (not 'aid'!) and loans were given not on the basis of fiscal soundness but solely on the basis of need, they would have a very different pattern and impact (Brandt, 1980, 1983). Once the existing framework of economic assumptions is questioned, consequential deliberation may lead in yet further directions. It might, for example, endorse not merely lobbying for a return to the fundamental purposes of international and other aid and development institutions, but working for their replacement by more effective institutions which are less responsive to the interests of the developed world (Brandt, 1980, 1983; IGBA, 1983). At this point we have sufficient reason to go back to more theoretical consideration of consequential reasoning to discover why it has produced such strong disagreements about what ought to be done.

The source of these disagreements does not lie in the structure of consequentialist reasoning, considered in the abstract. As a pattern of thought, consequentialism promises both wide scope and precise resolution of problems. If disagreements between consequentialists have been common, this shows that at least some of what is needed to make consequentialist reasoning action-guiding and accessible for agents and agencies who are placed to do something is missing. The most frequent concerns of consequentialists themselves are that we lack *either* precise ways of making interpersonal utility comparisons (so cannot *really* work out the aggregate benefit of acts or policies) *or* sufficient causal knowledge to support the instrumental reasoning that consequential deliberations may need. However, it might also be that we lack ways of finding out how the problems we face should best be described or which acts or policies are available in actual contexts of deliberation, or that the proposed decision procedures or algorithms of consequentialist thinking fail to capture matters of ethical importance. These possibilities will be considered in this and the next chapter, beginning with a look at the central difficulties of calculating benefit and reckoning consequences.

4   Calculating Benefit: Accuracy and Precision

Bentham's felicific calculus supposedly offered a method for determining expected utility which was not only generally accurate, but quite precise. Seven different dimensions of utility were to be taken into account; and lest we forget any in our calculation of benefits he provided a mnemonic verse (Bentham, 1789, Vol. I, p. 16):

> *Intense, long, certain, speedy, fruitful, pure,* –
> Such marks in *pleasures* and in pains endure.
> Such pleasures seek if *private* be thy end:
> If it be *public*, wide let them *extend*.

The aspiration for precision has been widely rejected by later utilitarians, although still pursued (at least in theoretical discussions) by some economists and decision-theorists. Mill's view that distinct sorts of pleasures were incommensurable undercut the basis of supposedly arithmetic summing of pleasures, since different pleasures might have to be measured in irreducibly different units. Yet Mill too supposed that broadly accurate judgements of the likely benefit of different actions and policies could be reached. This view is shared by many later utilitarian writers on ethics. They take a broadly humane rather than a precise and scientific view of judgements of utility, and stress that these are all that we can or need to make for ethical deliberation.

However, doing without *precision* is one thing and doing without *accuracy* is another. Action can certainly be guided by principles that discriminate only rather broad categories of action,[3] but the Principle of Utility would offer not so much ethical guidance as misguidance if its assessment of the goodness of results were not just imprecise but inaccurate.

Since consequentialists, including utilitarians, disagree radically over famine and world hunger, we must take seriously the thought that *one* source of disagreement may be lack of an accurate method for judging benefits. The source of disagreements *might* lie elsewhere. They might, for example, be due to disputes about the causal connections, and resulting uncertainty either about the likely outcome of available actions or about the best way to produce some accurately identified benefit. Still, one difficulty might be simply that we lack methods for identifying benefits accurately.

A reasonable starting point for considering what it takes to identify expected benefits with some accuracy might work from our own case. We may be pretty sure that hunger hurts, and that the security of knowing where future meals are coming from is a major source of ease and that this will be the same for others. However, the disagreements between rival consequentialist approaches to problems of famine and hunger have not been about the uncontentious benefit of not being hungry, but about the relative benefits of different global approaches to that goal. Malthusian *laissez faire* and a wide variety of planned development strategies are each thought by their proponents to minimize the suffering of unrelieved hunger. Such disagreements may reflect only divergent views about the likely results of different approaches to hunger and famine; but they might also reveal a general difficulty over judging benefits. Can we extrapolate convictions about what we would experience as benefits or harms in familiar contexts to form global judgements?

Utilitarian judgements of benefit which are not grounded in a Benthamite account of measurable pains and pleasures are *subjective* in two closely related senses. Benefits are always benefits *to some subject*. *Results* are what they are whether or not they are seen or experienced under some description by those whom they affect. However, nothing is a *benefit*, or a *harm*, in utilitarian thinking, unless seen or experienced as such by some subject (Schick, 1982).[4] Secondly, the view that some result constitutes a benefit or a harm to some subject may not be generally shared; it may be a *merely subjective* view. A result may or may not meet someone's need or constitute an element of some supposedly objective conception of the good life; but anything which is not seen as a benefit (or harm) by a particular subject just is not a benefit (or harm) to him or her. Hence, where subjects have very different desires or preferences or value results variously, utilitarians must take these as the basis for calculations. As soon as we go beyond a very general comparison of the harm of being hungry with the benefit of being adequately fed, the subjective basis of 'humane' utilitarian reasoning leads to uncertainty about what others would find a benefit or harm, so makes it hard to reach stable conclusions.

Everybody no doubt prefers secure food supplies to hunger; but some people do not prefer the means to food security to continuing ways of life that make them vulnerable to hunger or even to famine. They may dislike and even reject the sorts of food that are offered as food 'aid'; they may prefer traditional ways of life even where these keep agricultural productivity low; they may prefer the larger families that perhaps worsen poverty. Utilitarian reasoning supposedly takes such preferences seriously. While it may endorse overriding others' autonomy for the sake of greater expected benefit, it is supposedly unpaternalistic in its approach to identifying and calculating benefit. Even recent and sophisticated forms of utilitarianism, which advocate distribution-sensitive ranking principles, are subjective in both these senses (Scheffler, 1982, ch. II). Utilitarianism is ultimately committed to the claim that what is right will vary with 'preferences that are not fixed but fluid' (Hare, 1981, p. 226): there are no acts which could not become obligatory given an appropriate shift in preferences.

If we could devise and operate a felicific calculus, actual expectations of benefit and harm of those affected could be scientifically measured and amalgamated; but it is one thing to invent such calculi, and another to apply them. In the abstract discussions of rational choice theory, there is ample precision and ingenuity in the calculation of hypothetical benefits. However, judgements of actual benefit and harm in utilitarian discussions of determinate contexts leave large scope for subjective and impressionistic claims about what others would consider to be benefit or harm.

We are well enough aware of ways in which ignorance and chauvinism can affect thinking about distant and unfamiliar parts of the world. Western views of the now-undeveloped countries have often been prejudiced and Eurocentric. How then can ethical deliberations about Third-World hunger and poverty be purged of ethnocentrism and of other idiosyncrasies and prejudices? Can utilitarian deliberation be freed of these? Is this not likely to be hard in deliberation which relies on a theory of value based on subjective preferences, and a decision procedure which determines social benefit by aggregating expected individual benefits? Although utilitarian thinking apparently rests on a broad and uncontentious view of agency, it is deeply committed to the individualism that has been central to modern European thought.

Even those who find such commitments uncontentious and justifiable would think utilitarian deliberating false to itself if it did not reject ethnocentric and politically or ideologically alien accounts of benefits or harms to others. If the assessment of benefit and harm is dominated by the perspective of the assessor rather than determined by that of the subject of the benefit or harm, the whole point of the utilitarian enterprise would be undercut, and utilitarian modes of thinking would tend to be infected by egoism. For this reason the repeated reports from those working for international and voluntary aid and development organizations of ways in which donors' views of aid projects tend to dominate recipients' views (McNeill, 1981; IGBA, 1983; Shawcross, 1984) is particularly worrying for utilitarians. The utilitarian slogan 'everybody to count for one, nobody for more than one' (J. S. Mill, 1861, p. 319; Bentham, 1789, Vol. I, p. 2) means that nobody has authority to determine what shall constitute a benefit or a harm for others. Attempts to determine others' good by considering what they *ought* to find a benefit reject utilitarianism and covertly depend on some other mode of ethical reasoning. Utilitarian reasoning has to begin with the expectations of utility of actual individuals.

In thinking about problems of poverty and hunger we are then faced with a dilemma. Either we take it that somehow broadly accurate knowledge is available and that information about preferences can be gathered and used in utilitarian deliberations, or we have to rely very much on hunch and impression, and *our* sense of what others would experience as benefit or harm. We are likely to find that others do not want hunger or destitution, but we cannot simply assume that they would accept our more specific views about what might constitute a benefit. We cannot conclude that those in an underdeveloped region who would find food a benefit would also view a whole gamut of modernizing and reforming schemes as benefit. In utilitarian thinking no priority attaches to those benefits which meet needs. Rather, it is the intensity of individuals' preferences and desires that gives them weight. Whenever people are deeply attached to arrangements and forms of life which stand in the way of improving their access to food and to other necessities, these preferences must have preponderant weight in utilitarian deliberations.

In a good deal of utilitarian writing the corollaries of starting with a subjective theory of value are blurred. When precise calculations of expected benefit and harm are unavailable it can seem plausible to *assume* that the poor would care most about secure food supplies, shelter, clean water, education and medical services and other basic needs. Such assumptions help to lead humane utilitarian deliberations in directions which seem plausible and coherent, but part of that plausibility is borrowed from whatever other (ethical?) outlook provides the assumption that the destitute care most about basic needs. Utilitarian thinkers have often grown up with other ethical traditions, which (perhaps fortunately) shape their claims about what is 'really' preferred. We can expect utilitarian reasoning of those whose moral education has instilled good preferences to lead to good results. The just and benevolent are likely to reach admirable conclusions even when they place their reasoning in a utilitarian frame (cf. Hirsch, 1976, pp. 11, 137–151; MacIntyre, 1981, chs 3–5). However, utilitarians who took the *real* preferences of the destitute seriously might find many who care as much (or more) about land, caste, tribe, traditional ways of life and religious affiliations as they do about material needs. Also they might find others whose basic needs could not weigh heavily in utilitarian deliberation because destitution had produced apathy. Policies whose benefits are not immediately visible may not be preferred to others with slighter but more palpable benefits. Acute need matters in utilitarian thinking only when it is perceived as harm.

This startling result is just one of a number of corollaries of starting from a subjective account of value. If the moral acceptability of action depends upon desires or preferences, as it does in all utilitarian thinking, then shifts in desires or preferences will alter optimal outcomes, and so alter claims about obligations. There is no vantage point from which shifts in desire can be evaluated or criticized – except where other desires are preponderant. Selfless, self-indulgent, selfish and vindictive desires and preferences must all be weighed in calculating aggregate benefit or harm, and will affect which act or policy is judged optimal. So must 'adaptive' and imposed and ignorant preferences (Elster, 1982). Even if some of the more counter-intuitive results of utilitarian deliberation might be avoided by relying on a 'distribution-sensitive' ranking principle, still any conceivable act or policy would become optimal given *some* conceivable shift of desires or preferences. Even action involving torture, barbarity, sadism, or deliberate starvation and extermination, could be judged wrong only when alternative available actions lead to better outcomes given actual desires or preferences. These distressing possibilities afflict not only abstracted utilitarian reasoning, but also more limited attempts to work out which particular sacrifices and harms may or may not be incurred for the sake of better futures. Some of these will be considered in discussing utilitarian justice.

In one way it is a merit in utilitarian thinking that it does not shrink from tough-minded calculation of costs that must be incurred if benefits are to be achieved. Nevertheless, by including *all* desires and preferences within its scope, utilitarian thinking can (surprisingly) end up paying scant attention to *any* actual desires or preferences. This arises because there is no temporal limit restricting utilitarian calculation of expected benefit to present desires or preferences. Unconcern for the actual preferences of the poor and hungry can be justified within a utilitarian way of thought, despite its subjective theory of value. The utilitarian commitment to considering the actual preferences of all who are or may be affected by some action or policy must take account of future preferences, both of those immediately affected and of those to be born (possibly in part as a result of such acts and policies) who will also be affected. In the long run all present preferences are likely to be outweighed by future preferences, and so present preferences need not, after all, determine utilitarian calculation.

This line of thought raises a vast range of theoretically interesting problems and possibilities for utilitarian discussions, especially of possible population policies (Parfit, 1984). It also suggests that the acts and policies which maximize aggregate benefit may not be those that aim to maximize present preferences, but those which aim to maximize whatever preferences they bring into existence. Large-scale policies of social engineering and population planning can then receive retrospective utilitarian endorsement if the futures they bring into existence satisfy the preferences which arise in those futures. At the limit we can imagine not-so-brave new worlds in which social engineering produces only those preferences it can satisfy. In a less speculative framework we can see that utilitarian reasoning may easily find reasons for overlooking present preferences, provided it suggests that present difficulties and harms are the optimal route to a happier future. No generation or generations of sacrifice, no disregard of present preferences, can in principle be ruled out in utilitarian thinking if preferences are themselves subjective and malleable, and if future preferences are likely to outweigh the sum of present preferences.

The view that food is beneficial is uncontroversial, but cannot resolve differences about what more specific acts or policies would constitute benefits to those who are now hungry or risk future famine. Utilitarians disagree largely because they are attracted *both* to an abstract account of value that is precise but not applicable, *and* to a vaguer and more open approach to judging likely benefit and harm which is not simply imprecise but allows ill-founded impressions, ignorance and ethnocentrism, as well as nonutilitarian ethical thinking, to affect judgements of harm and of benefit. We are then torn between the unattainable rigour of felicific calculation and a pattern of reasoning so plastic that it appears to support varied and mutually exclusive claims about what would benefit or harm the destitute. The plausible and sensible ring of so many humane utilitarian discussions of famine and world hunger shows that utilitarian judgements of benefit and harm are sufficiently plastic to be open to a wide range of appealing ethical considerations. They are also open to considering how others might be benefited not by satisfying, but by changing or controlling their preferences. Particularly in reasoning about the far future and about a public or international domain of action, such openness is a danger. In any case, it can hardly count as a theoretical merit in humane utilitarianism, although it may (seen from some other ethical perspective) provide reason to rely on utilitarian modes of reasoning to persuade in specific contexts of action.

Notes

1 There are those who think this is a deficiency (Rawls, 1971, p. 24 ff.; Smart and Williams, 1973, pp. 116–117; Scheffler, 1982, chs 2 and 4). Chapters 6 to 8 will argue

that an account of agency, but not a narrowly individualist account, is needed for an adequate view of deliberation about public affairs.

2 For example, they propose ranking principles which give extra weight to the desires of the worst-off (e.g. 'distribution sensitive ranking principles', Scheffler, 1982, p. 76 ff.) or to procedures which are sensitive to the limitations of human calculating capacities (e.g. 'satisficing', Simon, 1957) or to setting some limit to the requirements of duty (e.g. 'avoiding "overload" of obligations', cf Fishkin, 1982; Kagan, 1984).

3 Indeed no principle could discriminate among all possible actions. If actions are individuated in terms of descriptions, which can be indefinitely extended, possible descriptions will be indefinitely extendable and so there can be no calculus of descriptions, hence no algorithmic principle for guiding actions. Put more traditionally, in terms that link with Kantian and Wittgensteinian treatment of the topic, rules cannot contain rules for their own application.

4 This point is compatible with the lack of a *strong* conception of individual subjects or agents in utilitarian thinking. Rawls is correct in claiming that 'utilitarianism does not take seriously the distinction between persons' (Rawls, 1971, p. 27). Although expected harms and benefits are to be identified and quantified from the viewpoint of subjects, their aggregation discounts the boundaries between persons. Utilitarian reasoning can be both subjective and impersonal!

5
Reckoning the Consequences

An absolute morality places a prepared grid upon conduct
and upon a person's activities and interests, and thereafter
one only tends to see the pieces of his conduct and life as they
are divided by lines on the grid. (Hampshire, 1978b, p. 40)

Genuine progress in international relations depends on
painstaking negotiations to reach agreed principles or legal
instruments; only these processes can produce a common
language to provide a basis for action. (Brandt, 1980, p. 262)

1 Abstract and Accessible Consequential Reasoning

Utilitarian disagreements are rooted in a subjective theory of the
good. Taken in the abstract, and in the schematic examples of
textbooks, the notion of maximal happiness is clear enough.
Taken in context, where we lack an adequate objective theory of
the good, and have no felicific calculus to discipline calculations
of benefit, utilitarian reasoning has to be based on a subjective and
impressionistic account of individual and of aggregate benefit.
Calculations of benefit and of harm are then readily shaped by the
attitudes of deliberators and so by established and establishment
views about what is (or ought to be) a benefit or a harm.
Utilitarianism can be combined with the varied grids of social,
economic and ethical categories under which different individuals, collectivities or institutions perceive their problems, the
available actions or policies, and their results. Utilitarian thinking
can then readily be deployed by aid and development experts,
by transnational executives, by national and international
bureaucracies as well as by individuals in the developed and the
underdeveloped world.

A pattern of deliberation which is so widely accessible has a
great advantage for ethical reasoning about distant poverty and

development. Yet it also risks complete assimilation to the standard categories of particular agents and agencies. There would be little practical (or philosophical) point in a theory of ethical deliberation which could neither check, challenge nor reject the categories of deliberation established in a given milieu. 'Normal' ethical deliberation does not need duplication. Utilitarian deliberation, however, risks assimilation to established and establishment categories of deliberation not only in calculating benefit, but in identifying ethical problems and reckoning the consequences of alternative lines of action and policies. The problem is to see how and whether consequentialist reasoning could be widely accessible yet not assimilable.

If consequential reasoning is to be used in contexts of action, and not just in discussions of abstract, hypothetical examples, it must be linked to empirical and causal knowledge. The former is needed to pick out or construe situations and problems that may need action; the latter is needed to determine what action or policies are available and their likely results. The close historical connection between social science and utilitarian thinking about problems of the public domain, including famines and poverty, is no accident. If social inquiry gives an accurate, objective view of problems of social life and their causal connections, utilitarians can rely on it for instrumental reasoning about public problems.

If utilitarians could know the results of various development policies, they could (after calculating which benefit is optimal) reckon which ought to be pursued and which rejected. A second explanation of the deep disagreements among consequentialists who have written on famine and world hunger might then be that development studies have not yet provided accurate knowledge of problems, policies and their results. This explanation appeals to those who expect advances in social science to produce the missing knowledge.

For example, Singer (1979, pp. 175–178) and others have suggested that neo-Malthusian perspectives on development can now be rejected because social inquiry has shown that population growth does not automatically continue until resources are exhausted, and that this shows that *laissez faire* policies towards the Third World are not optimal. Those policies will certainly produce unnecessary deaths, and it has not been shown that they will prevent even more unnecessary deaths. Others think that even if *particular* neo-Malthusian claims (such as Hardin's view that giving aid raises birth rates) have been rebutted, there has been no general rebuttal of such views. Social inquiry has not shown that interventionist policies would never fuel runaway population growth. However, anybody who is optimistic about discovering laws of social change will expect utilitarian deliberations to lead to increasingly accurate recommendations for action on a broadening spectrum of social issues. Meanwhile, 'moral philosophers who are consequentialists explain . . . away contrary moral claims as uncertainty about outcomes' (Hampshire, 1978b, p. 44).

Utilitarians of Benthamite and of humane persuasions will, of course, differ over the precision with which instrumental reasoning based on social science can or need guide action. If benefit could be calculated with Benthamite precision, utilitarian deliberating could yield similarly precise recommendations *if* it also drew on accurate knowledge of social causes and effects. However, if judgements of relative benefit are only approximate, no amount of detailed knowledge of means to various results, or results of various policies, could make precise calculation of optimal benefits possible. The conclusions of utilitarian deliberations will not be more precisely articulated than the least precise link in the chain. Nevertheless, humane utilitarians too expect advances in social science to produce causal knowledge to underpin their instrumental reasoning. At least, they may hope, systematic social inquiry can sometimes show that proposed action or policies will not lead to the results that are claimed for them. At best, humane utilitarians too may hope that social science will provide a foundation for social engineering, just as natural science provides one for physical engineering.

If this optimism is to be justified, two conditions must be met. Most fundamentally, social science must provide the required empirical and causal knowledge. Secondly, this knowledge must be accessible to those who start with the standard grids of categories of agents and agencies who deliberate about major changes of the sort that can affect the risk of famine and the continuation of poverty and hunger. Both conditions are demanding.

Much deliberation about hunger and development is, indeed, located in institutions that use patterns of consequential reasoning. International agencies often evaluate proposed development loans on the basis of explicit comparisons of the benefits of alternative aid projects. More or less formalized and detailed comparisons of costs and benefits of alternative lines of action are commonly made in many different commercial and policy-making institutions. Some individual agents may use, and more may understand, consequential ways of selecting styles of life, lines of employment or ways of using surplus income.

However, the very institutions, practices and habits of life which secure the accessibility of consequential reasoning in some contexts also restrict its impact. Institutions are not responsive to consequential reasoning in general, but to consequential reasoning that fits their working practices and mandate. For example, if a development loan is to be evaluated in consequential terms it will be judged and assessed under specific headings, to see whether this proposed use of funds is indeed optimal (or at least better than other proposed uses) in terms of a limited grid of categories which are embodied in the working practices of a particular institution. In some cases these may be purely commercial criteria – How secure is the loan? Will it be repaid? What rate of interest can be negotiated? Consequential reasoning of this sort is hardly to be thought of as *ethical* reasoning, since the conception of benefit used is that of commercial advantage to the loan-making institution. In other cases a wider range of results may be considered. 'Soft' loans are made at lower than commercial rates of interest, and may be evaluated in terms of a grid which includes some noncommercial categories – Is the project feasible? Is it likely to contribute to over-all development in the recipient country? Will it contribute to employment and to the exports of the recipient country? More questionably, will it contribute to the political objectives, or the exports, of the 'donor' country? Proposals for food aid too will be evaluated in terms of their contribution to specific outcomes.

The categories used by institutions whose decisions affect aid, trade and development policies vary. Concern for 'donor' interests is often embodied in the formal mandate and in the working practices of bilateral 'aid' programmes (Wallerstein, 1980; Dinham and Hines, 1983; Shawcross, 1984). Concern for commercial viability and profit is likely to dominate the charters and practices of banks, commodity brokers and transnational corporations (Morgan, 1979; Dinham and Hines, 1983). Concern for meeting various standards of effectiveness, noncorruption and 'good management' is widespread. A commitment to meeting needs is dominant in some fundamental international documents, but less so in the working practices of some international agencies (McNeill, 1981; Shawcross, 1984). Concern for maximal control over aid resources may be common to 'donor' and recipient governments and other agencies. Many of these concerns are institutionalized in the charters and working practices of institutions. In the end it is consequential reasoning conducted *within these constraints* rather than consequential reasoning in the abstract that guides aid and development decisions. In the process, unsurprisingly, some problems and policies which would be important in comprehensive consequential reasoning, are neglected, and others which might appear rather trivial in a more global reckoning of consequences are emphasized. One recent critic (see McNeill, 1981, p. 85; cf. Shue, 1980, ch. 7) of aid policies and decisions suggests that many problems are

> attributable not to incompetence or corruption but to the machinery of aid, the 'rules of the game', which have been devised by donors in such a way as to allow them to continue to exercise leverage.

He advocates, as do many others, changes in the 'rules of the game' so that institutions which make aid and development decisions can come closer to the decisions that would be reached in unrestricted consequential reasoning. McNeill's suggestion (1981, pp. 85–86) is that

> Instead of slowly conceding ground with regard to specific 'rules of the game', is it not time to allow aid recipients a voice in drawing up the rules? . . . So long as the aid relationship is unequal and control remains with the donors only relatively minor changes . . . may be realistically considered.

Similar criticisms of current institutional practice and suggestions for improvements are made by many others (Brandt, 1980, 1983; Hoffmann, 1981, ch. 4; Sen, 1981; IGBA, 1983). In general, the complaint is that even institutions set up to help the Third World have been too responsive to powerful interests and, at their worst, counter-productive. They have promoted the political and commercial interests of richer nations. They have sponsored development projects that do not benefit the poorest, have undercut the viability of subsistence farming by dumping subsidized surplus food, and encouraged vulnerable production for export markets to which access has not been guaranteed (Jackson, 1982; Dinham and Hines, 1983). They have failed to tackle underlying social and economic structures which leave the poor without means to buy food, and have responded as though famine reflected only a shortage of available food (Sen, 1981). It is tempting to think that a progressive reform of 'rules of the game' could replace the restricted consequential reasoning which now guides the policies of aid and development agencies with unrestricted consequential reasoning. Why should not the grid of categories used by such agencies be revised to detect and respond to broader ranges of problems? Why should not such changes also transform individuals' consequential deliberation? Individual action cannot either help or harm the distant poor unless mediated by institutions such as banks, transnational corporations, national governments and multinational agencies, or international or voluntary organizations. Even so simple an action as trying to send money to an individual in the Third World is constrained by banking and currency regulations, by the development of postal services and literacy, and by the prevalence of corruption. Even seeking work which benefits some of the poorest may end in frustration if the 'rules of the game' of a particular (international or voluntary) organization do not permit response to various sorts of predicament (Shawcross, 1984). What count as 'problems' for any individual and the repertoire of actions available to him or her will be limited by the mandate and practices – the 'rules of the game' – of the institutions that mediate those actions. If the range of individuals' consequential deliberation is to be widened, the 'rules of the game' of institutions which mediate their action will have to be changed to allow a wider range of situations to count as *problems* and an appropriate range of actions to be considered as *solutions*.

Changing the 'rules of the game' is always a difficult matter. It is a strength of the utilitarian tradition that it has always seen the need for this level of response too. Bentham's most celebrated work is, after all, an introduction to the principles of *Legislation* as well as of *Morals*. The task of the utilitarian legislator is to redesign the institutions of society so that their 'normal', rule-governed operation will respond to problems and generate decisions, actions and policies just as unrestricted, unmediated utilitarian consideration of particular cases would. If a utilitarian legislator does this well the gap between act and rule utilitarian calculations about particular cases will lessen. The dilemma of the individual agent whose action must be mediated by structures which subvert its aim will be minimized. Those who seek to help the poor and hungry through their work would not have to fear that their action would be fruitless. Those who try to send money to the neediest would not have to fear that it would be diverted by corrupt officials or damage the economy of a vulnerable region and so harm the neediest. Other changes might ensure that institutional action did not end up benefiting 'donor' agencies or nations rather than recipients, and commercial practices might be regulated in ways that ensured that the operations of markets benefited rather than harmed the neediest.

Clearly, any utilitarian legislator who could so redesign social institutions would make a very great contribution to human happiness. However, if we are committed to *accessible* practical reasoning, we can have no quick recourse to utilitarian legislators. No actual ruler or legislator or lesser institution is a utilitarian legislator. Actual individuals and institutions all have interests and priorities other than maximizing human happiness. Whatever institutions and practices they advocate or work for will reflect their 'rules of the game'. The utilitarian legislator is a vivid characterization of a hypothetical perspective from which benefit to each would be weighed without selective perception of problems or restricted repertoires of response or limited knowledge. The legislator, like Rousseau's grand cosmopolitan spirit and various ideal moral spectators, is no more than a gesture towards a locus where complete ethical reasoning – in Bentham's case utilitarian reasoning – is conducted. Accessible ethical argument cannot address a vacant and abstract locus, but must reach actual agents and agencies whose perceptions of problems, possibilities for action and knowledge of causes will be restricted in definite ways. Such accessible reasoning may fail to identify actions which would be judged optimal in the abstract, but abstracted reasoning may fail to reach the agents and agencies who can make a difference. We can no more rely on actual social agents or agencies being utilitarian legislators than we can rely on kings being philosophers. The problem is not just the often-cited difficulty of finding actual agents or agencies with wholly benevolent motivation, but the unavoidable lack of agents or agencies with the required 'neutral' grid of categories. Accessible ethical reasoning arises only in actual social contexts, where agents and agencies not only have limited benevolence, but depend on a limited cognitive repertoire, which defines the problems and the sorts of reasoning which they find salient. Hence we must think of the categories and practices of actual agencies and other institutions not only as *constraints* on accessible deliberation and action, but also as *enabling* some sorts of considerations to be accessible to those whose action may make a difference. The grid of categories embodied in the laws and practices of a given society or institution is not simply an obstacle to accessible utilitarian deliberation, but essential for it.

If accessible practical reasoning has to take place within enabling constraints, it is bound to have difficulty in criticizing the institutions and practices whose grid of categories constitute the constraints. When the very identification of problems, of available action and policies and of their likely results presupposes the terms of reference of certain institutions, those presuppositions will be carried into any deliberation that is accessible to the institution or to individuals and collectivities whose actions are mediated by the institution. It seems that utilitarian reasoning must either be abstract and inaccessible to actual agents and agencies, or else embody the presuppositions and hence the limitations of those agents and agencies. Accessible reasoning apparently has to accept the status quo, and unrestricted utilitarian reasoning has to remain inaccessible. This may have serious implications for utilitarian deliberation about problems which, like those of world hunger and poverty, are seen in conflicting ways from different social perspectives.

2   Utilitarian Deliberation and Social Criticism

On this account utilitarian ethical reasoning must either be abstract and inaccessible – or accessible but uncritical of established and establishment grids of categories. This conclusion may seem not only unwelcome, but implausible in the light of the radical crusades of the early utilitarians. Surely the effective advocates of so many schemes for social and legal reform and improvement, ranging from factory acts and penal reform to extension of the franchise, cannot have been prisoners of established modes of discourse? Nor do the early utilitarians seem to have been as disunited in views of optimal action and policies as their successors appear to be in disarray about approaches to world hunger and development. Is there then some further feature of utilitarian thinking that gives it a critical edge, and enables it to look beyond current categories of discourse? Or do the radical successes of early utilitarian thinking reflect particular features of the period and social context in which it flourished (Hampshire, 1978a)?

This historical hypothesis is in some ways plausible. The fundamental categories of utilitarian thought were well established in some modes of discussion and aspects of life by the turn of the eighteenth century, but still absent in others. Human life was at times described in individualistic and market terms; at other times more traditional social categories prevailed. An example of this confrontation can be found in the contrast between Paine's championship of the Rights of Man, and Burke's insistence that there are no rights of individual men, but only the time-honoured and established rights – the 'normal' rights – of particular human collectivities. Paine's defence of abstract individual rights did not gain utilitarian assent. Bentham notoriously remarked that the doctrine of natural rights was no more than 'nonsense upon stilts' (Bentham, n.d., ch. II, p. 501). However, the sticking-point was not Paine's individualism, which Bentham largely shared, as did Mill, who later domesticated an account of individual rights for utilitarian use. The early utilitarians argued in a social and intellectual context in which individualist thinking was no longer wholly alien nor yet wholly established, and conceptions of rights embodying different attitudes to individualism coexisted. In that context of debate utilitarian argument could be accessible to agents and agencies who were already versed in individualist ways of thought, yet radical in its rejection of persisting laws and customs that endorsed forms of privilege and denied the individualist claim that 'everybody should count for one'.

For parallel reasons, deliberation based on a subjective theory of value could both gain access to ears already attuned to the thought that individual impressions had some epistemological authority, yet have radical implications for forms of life still imbued with respect for traditional laws and institutions with scant regard for the impressions of the unprivileged. *In this particular historical context* utilitarian arguments could both be accessible to relevant agents and agencies and have radical implications. The success of these arguments in fostering individualist conceptions of human life and subjective conceptions of value, and institutions which embody both conceptions, diminished the radical potential of utilitarian thought. As more and more social institutions were refashioned to respond to individual desires and preferences, arguments based on those desires and preferences were less likely to challenge the status quo. Once an extended franchise makes the political order responsive to individual preferences, and market structures produce an analogously responsive economic system, utilitarian modes of thought are likely to support the status quo in fundamental ways. Their very success makes them strands in a dominant rather than a critical ideology. Where many social institutions share the fundamental assumptions and categories of utilitarian thinking, such thinking is likely to provide only limited criticism of existing institutions and their policies. This is the price of success.

Many contemporary utilitarians would dispute this diagnosis. They do not think that the critical, even radical demands of early utilitarians were due to special historical circumstances. They would contend that utilitarian ways of thinking retain the potential for fundamental criticism of institutions and policies whenever these are less than optimal ways of achieving human happiness. They would point out that much recent utilitarian writing on problems of famine and world hunger has advocated quite radical changes of action and policy. Peter Singer's advocacy of dramatically increased giving to the poor is a case in point; so is Hardin's advocacy of a *laissez faire* approach to the destitute. They would also insist that, since small changes in actions and policies may greatly alter results, and with them benefits and harms, utilitarian reasoning will always have the critical task of monitoring current action and proposals and reviewing claims that certain actions or policies are beneficial or optimal. Certainly, utilitarians will not criticize arrangements which they do not think need improving; but they will not be restricted to minor criticism of established institutions and policies.

However, utilitarian thought *today* cannot base a reputation for critical capacities just on the diversity of its current proposals and an honourable history of radical criticism. Some present disagreements may be relatively superficial; but others may be symptoms of ways of thought too plastic to resolve difficult cases, which they leave open to impression and subjectivity. Utilitarians do not, however, regard their accounts of problems and of available actions, or their reckoning of consequences, as imprisoned by established modes of discourse, and so would deny that critical utilitarian thinking needs special historical circumstances.

Subjectivity is supposed to have a *basic* but *limited* role in utilitarian thinking. Subjective judgements of benefit and harm are supposed to provide the *basis* for claims about the value of different states of affairs; yet these subjective elements are themselves to be measured, compared and aggregated and then pursued or shunned with unsubjective rigour. Expert and objective technique is to be applied to subjective starting points. Outside limited contexts of personal life, these calculations depend on expertise whose cultivation and pursuit itself demands certain sorts of social institutions.

To provide this expertise, utilitarian thinking has consistently advocated social structures which provide objectivity and criticism where it is needed. The career open to talents, which utilitarians have always advocated, was not only a structure by which work and employment could better be organized to accommodate individual desires or preferences; it was also a means for producing the *cadres* of experts and planners, of technocrats and social scientists, of economists, criminologists and bureaucrats without whom the efficient delineation of problems and options, and calculation and pursuit of optimal ends could not proceed. However, what guarantees that the expertise of the *cadres* is as independent and objective as their role in utilitarian deliberation requires? Will not officials and experts who are to diagnose problems, chart available courses of action and reveal connections between available action and preferred results in the public domain have their own preferences, their own agenda of priorities and grid of categories? May they not (unlike early utilitarian radicals) lack shared categories that can make reasoning which criticizes established institutions and practices accessible to the relevant audiences?

The ideal civil servant supposedly pursues the varied ends proposed by successive political masters with impartial efficiency. The utilitarian expert, though not indeed an idealized legislator, is supposed to pursue aggregate happiness with dispassionate zeal. However, actual experts who try to make utilitarian calculations about far-reaching policies, such as might improve the prospects of the Third World, must use established categories and institutions. How then can they produce neutral and objective accounts of problems, possible action, and expected utilities, and calculate optimal outcomes? If actual experts and officials are constrained by the categories of their personal and professional formation, and by the terms of their office, this will limit the critical capacities of utilitarian reasoning.

This problem is supposedly met by ensuring that the educational and professional formation of officials and experts, and their terms of reference, are not narrowly sectoral. Officials and experts in the modern, developed world are expected to be neutral and objective in many *specific* ways, which guarantee their detachment from the outlook and interests of any one section of society. Professionals are trained to assess particular cases impartially and objectively. Civil servants are required to deal even-handedly with members of the public, to refuse bribes and preference, and discount their own political views. In many countries members of the armed forces are held to traditions of political impartiality. Above all the judiciary is required to keep to standards of unbiased fairness. Nepotism and corruption are always unacceptable. Failure to meet these standards is taken seriously and is concealed and denied even where common. The development of cadres of officials and experts capable of setting aside both personal perceptions and preference and the demands of family, friends and ethnic group, lends some plausibility to the utilitarian vision of experts who impartially identify problems, formulate policies, reckon the consequences and calculate benefits.

There are two aspects to the formation of impartial experts. Utilitarians can indeed explain the importance of finding experts whose *motivation* is impartial. All of us prefer to be dealt with by professionals and officials who are *not* influenced by idiosyncratic or personal preferences. Perhaps a wholly utilitarian society would have difficulty producing experts who were motivationally neutral; indeed, it may seem paradoxical that utilitarian reasoning, which seeks to aggregate and satisfy subjective preferences, should need officials and professionals whose practical reasoning follows a different pattern (see Hirsch, 1976, p. 11):

> A critical omission from this approach is the role played by the supporting ethos of social obligation in the formulation of the relevant public policies . . . the principle of self interest is incomplete as a social organizing device . . . the deeper irony – which can also be seen as a fortunate legacy – resides in the success of the market system in its initial phase, on the shoulders of a premarket social ethos. A system that depends for its success on a heritage that it undermines cannot be sustained on the record of its bountiful fruits.

Utilitarians may reply that, even if this account is accurate – and it is a matter of historical good fortune that there continue to be those who can and will administer and advise impartially – still this is our actual situation. For the present, utilitarian social and economic policies can rely on these cadres and their anachronistic professional ethos. If and when the heritage is squandered, other means for embodying utilitarian patterns of deliberation in institutional structures must be found. When the heritage runs out a utilitarian future will have to depend more on explicit regulation of the cadres and less on a 'supporting ethos of social obligation'. The paradox is no deeper than the standard point that where utility is best brought about by following rules, the best rules may not demand that each act be determined by the principle of utility.

However, such debates about the ethos and *motivation* of officials and professionals are distractions from basic theoretical issues. Whether the administration of utilitarian policies lies in the hands of cadres of partially nonutilitarian motivation and formation, or whether it is regulated and enforced by explicit utilitarian codes and penalties, certain judgements and calculations must be made. Problems must be identified, available actions must be listed; preferences for possible outcomes must be discerned and aggregated; the optimal available action must be picked out and pursued. Utilitarian deliberation requires experts who have not just appropriate motivation, but appropriate, 'neutral' *cognitive* structures. The deeper problem is not *how* these cognitive structures can be guaranteed at a given time, but *whether* they can be secured at all. If they cannot, utilitarian deliberation will be confined to established categories of thought.

The limited motivational neutrality that is actually available in fortunate circumstances does not in the least guarantee that experts and officials approach problems and situations with neutral categories. They are supposed, on the contrary, to bring professional categories and expertise and not blank neutrality to the affairs that they handle. They are supposedly equipped with a finer grid of categories, and not a *tabula rasa*. This is why professional formation takes a long time. It is also why expert cognitive limitations rather than expert motivation are the serious obstacle to expert neutrality.

3   Instrumental Reasoning and Social Science

Expert advice might be in principle available and yet universally (or at least widely) accessible if it could be formulated in a universally accessible vocabulary. If a *science of society* could provide a value-neutral and universally accessible account of social reality, experts who relied on it could identify problems and policies and reckon results in value-neutral ways. They could provide the instrumental reasoning which utilitarian deliberation needs if it is neither to be abstract (so inaccessible and unable to guide action), nor accessible only to those confined within some mode of 'normal' political and ethical discourse. However, if there is no science of society, experts may also fail to deliver (Rorty, 1983, pp. 161–162; cf. Taylor, 1982; Schick, 1982):

> Suppose we picture the 'value-free' social scientist walking up to the divide between 'fact' and 'value' and handing predictions to the policy makers who live on the other side. They will not be of much use unless they contain some of the terms that the policy makers use among themselves. What the policy makers would like, presumably, are rich juicy predictions, like 'If basic industry is socialized, the standard of living will (or won't) decline', 'if literacy is made more widespread, more honest people will be elected to office', and so on. They would like hypothetical sentences whose consequents are phrased in the terms that might occur in

morally urgent recommendations. When they get predictions phrased in the sterile jargon of 'quantified' social sciences ('maximizes satisfactions', 'increases conflict') they are quite right to tune out. The only sort of policy makers who would be receptive to what presently passes for 'behavioural science' would be the rulers of the Gulag or of Huxley's *Brave New World*, or a conspiracy of those who personify Foucault's forces of domination

The dilemma is pointed. The vocabulary of action which is accessible to agents and agencies – which they understand, follow and find appropriate – is not universally or widely accessible; and the 'thin' vocabulary which is fairly widely accessible is not useful for the deliberations of actual agents and agencies. Rorty's picture queries whether there is universally accessible instrumental reasoning about social institutions which has any weight or significance. If there is none, utilitarian ethical deliberation about distant problems, like poverty and hunger, which are affected by many agents and agencies, seems doomed. Such deliberation needs to be widely accessible, but cannot be so if the relevant agents and agencies have no common grid of categories.

However, Rorty might be mistaken. Surely there is a reasonably 'thick' and widely shared vocabulary of action. The vocabulary of national and international politics and law and some economic terms are widely shared. However, a shared vocabulary may not be enough basis for universally or widely accessible instrumental reasoning (Hoffman, 1981, p. 20).

A community of vocabulary is not the same thing as a community of values. When people with very different values use the same vocabulary, it debases both the vocabulary and the values hidden behind the vocabulary. That is what has happened to notions like self-determination and non-intervention, etc. Behind the common grammar there are competing ideologies

Sometimes there either is no shared social and economic vocabulary, or only one that expresses a grid of categories which seems blind, insensitive or even corrupt. Hoffman's point about the terms 'self-determination' and 'non-intervention' could be repeated for many of the terms most used in discussions of world

hunger and poverty. There are divergent understandings of central notions in development studies. Development itself is seen as
economic growth alone by some, but as including political and
social transformations by others (Brandt, 1980, 1983; Harrison,
1981). Conceptions of boundaries and of the significant descriptions of regions which are underdeveloped are equally varied.
Even geographical and historical description can be contentious.
Eurocentrism penetrates the very mapping of the Third World,
whose size shrinks in the commonly used Mercator projection,
while that of the 'North' is exaggerated. It is evident in the
common view that populous non-European lands were 'discovered' by European explorers. These biases are more readily
detected and corrected than the pervasive use of some rather than
other social and economic categories. Economic growth may be
seen as progress or as exploitation, as development or as neo-
colonialism, political movements as subversion or as national
liberation.

The main obstacle to the neutral expertise which utilitarian
deliberation about global problems needs is not that experts and
officials in fact lack the benevolent motivation of abstract utilitarian legislators (though no doubt they often do). It is that their
instrumental reasoning unavoidably deploys one or another
specific grid of categories which is partly alien to many agents and
agencies whose action is needed.

Utilitarian deliberations about development policies and
responses to world hunger and the risk of famine face a startling
dilemma. The causal generalizations of global scope that social
scientists may discover cannot be formulated in terms of a
universally accessible grid of categories, since the universally
accessible categories are too 'thin' and general. Global generalizations will not therefore be accessible to all agents or agencies, but
(at best) to those who understand the categories and idiom of
social science, and take these to be appropriate. Hence the various
experts, the social scientists and those individuals and institutions
who share their idiom, are the only possible agents and agencies
of large-scale changes to whom full utilitarian reasons can be
given. In this picture utilitarian deliberations about global problems are unavoidably *de haut en bas*; the development projects
and policies which are endorsed by such reasoning will not be
those which emerge 'from the grass roots', but rather the 'top-
down' projects which expert deliberation pronounces optimal

(Berger, 1974; Harrison, 1981; Jackson, 1982). Since instrumental reasoning which eschews agents' concepts must be inaccessible to those agents, expertise can only affect what is done when the experts not merely advise, but rule.

If, on the other hand, social inquiry produces only generalizations which use agents' categories, its findings may be accessible and of use to the agents and agencies it studies. However, in this case there can be no universally or even widely accessible social science, hence no over-all theory of development and social change. Discussions of the methods and philosophy of social science often claim that agents' concepts *must* provide the categories of social inquiry (Winch, 1958; Rorty, 1983). If only interpretive or hermeneutic theories of economic development and social change are possible, utilitarian deliberation which depends on these generalizations must be equally restricted in scope. There can be no global prescriptions about development or social change, but only the local and possibly conflicting prescriptions of 'normal' social and ethical debate. Agents or agencies whose social and economic categories diverged could not discuss development problems together, let alone agree on any global development policy. In such a picture, small may or may not be beautiful, but large is certainly illusory.

A lot of utilitarian deliberation on global problems embraces both horns of this dilemma. It assumes both that social science can provide global generalizations and hence use categories that are alien to many, and that it can ground instrumental reasoning that is widely accessible. However, utilitarian deliberators, like the rest of us, cannot have it both ways. If they think that there is or can be a complete, objective social science, then they must think that any instrumental reasoning based on that science is accessible only to experts, who have mastered and use the categories of that science. If they think that social inquiry is fundamentally hermeneutic or interpretive, they must treat any conceptual barriers between different agents and agencies as barriers to instrumental reasoning. In that case generally accessible reasoning about global problems, including famine and hunger and poverty, cannot be expected until there is a more generally shared outlook. Premature deliberations with global ambitions are inaccessible; they can only be heard once an appropriate ideological context has been established.

In spite of the many ways in which experts and officials may be free of personal bias and subjectivity, their independence from established social categories is neither likely nor – if they are to advise rather than to impose social policies – helpful. If utilitarian deliberation is to be critical of established grids of categories, it needs supplementing with a method for evaluating choices of social categories.

4   Value Neutrality and Consciousness Raising

Perhaps then the first step for utilitarian deliberators is to try to change received views so that the findings of social science become accessible beyond the groups of experts in whose idiom they are expressed. If the idiom of social science was spread, its findings would become accessible to more agents and agencies.

However, this suggestion leads to a further dilemma. If spreading the language and findings of social science is a *preliminary* to more widely accessible ethical deliberation, how could such action to transform others' grids of categories be justified? Even if the language of social science were a value-neutral idiom, spreading it might or might not be ethically uncontroversial. Not every transformation of consciousness raises consciousness (Berger, 1974, pp. 135–151). Spreading the language of social science might, for example, be a way in which the self-understanding and political effectiveness of those whose consciousness is purportedly raised is paralysed. Inducting others into a universal vocabulary of social analysis may be one more form of 'cognitive imperialism', and as much in need of justification as any other activity to change others' outlook and hence their action in basic ways.

In any case, it does not seem likely that much of the social science currently available in development studies (or perhaps elsewhere) is value neutral in the required sense. On the contrary, the categories which it uses are often hotly disputed, and the source of dispute is often that their use is dictated neither by the subject matter concerned, nor by 'mere' stipulation, but by undeclared ethical commitments. Social 'science' *as we know it* is not value neutral at all. Many of its theories are contested because they construe a domain of problems as having one rather than another configuration and so as being amenable to some but not to other ranges of action and policy. Many writers on the philosophical presuppositions of social science think that this is not due to any temporary or remediable backwardness in social studies, but an unavoidable feature of social inquiry (de Haan, 1983).

The categories of social science have often concealed ethically questionable positions in the past (see Hampshire, 1978b, p. 51):

An illusory image of rationality distorted the judgment of the American policy-makers. They thought that their opponents in the USA were sentimental and guided only by their unreflective emotions, while they, the policy-makers, were computing consequences with precision and objectivity, using quasi quantitative methods. They ignored, and remained insensitive to, the full nature and quality of their acts in waging war, and of the shame and odium attached to some particular acts. . . . Under the influence of bad social science, and the bad moral philosophy that usually goes with it, they over-simplified the moral issues and provided an example of false rationality.

Some of the social science which is invoked in development studies may also exemplify 'false rationality'. Two suggestive examples are the uses made of economic and nationalist categories of analysis.

By describing an economic situation in terms of standard categories of market economics we implicitly assume that certain acts or policies are uncontroversial interventions but others are questionable and in need of justification. As soon as holdings are described as the *property* of some *landowner* who *rents* them to *his tenants* we have more than a description of a set of property relations as they exist at a particular time and place. The description invites the question of whether the rents are *fair* or *too high*; but it suppresses the question of whether any rent can justly be charged, or whether certain sorts of tenancy might not simply be unjust. By using these and related categories as a starting point it can appear that reforms of land tenure arrangements raise the question of how *expropriation* should be *compensated* for. It may even appear that, since *expropriation* by definition takes what is somebody's *own*, it is patently unjust and so no just land reform scheme can rely on it. Using these categories, it is difficult to ask whether it is not *failure* to 'expropriate' without 'compensation' that is unjust.

A second example of the use of categories in development studies which tacitly import certain ethical assumptions can be found in the use of standard nationalist categories of analysis. Development studies are conducted to a great extent in terms of consideration of *national* needs and development. The level of Gross *National* Product is taken as an obvious measure of development. The powers of the *international* agencies are quite different from and derivative from those of *nations* and *national institutions. Redistributive taxation within a nation* is seen by many in principle as ethically uncontroversial, whereas *transnational redistribution financed from taxation* is usually thought highly controversial, an intrusion of legal coercion into what is properly the sphere of charity and of nationally determined 'aid' policies (Nagel, 1977; Shue, 1980, pp. 131 ff.). However much *abstract* ethical discussions proclaim that the boundaries of nations are not the real boundaries of moral concern (cf. Hoffmann, 1981; Lichtenberg, 1981), the very terms in which studies of development, aid and trade are conducted reveal that this is not the standard assumption in social 'science'. Even when care is taken not to treat nations as the only units for counting poverty or wealth, international redistribution and aid remain controversial in ways that domestic redistribution and welfare policies are not (Walzer, 1983, ch. 2).

One reason why the categories of market economics or of international relations can seem ethically uncontroversial is that they correspond to legal realities. They appear to offer straightforward descriptions. After all, it is uncontroversial that there are landlords and tenants in Bangladesh, and that the underdeveloped world consists of underdeveloped nations. However, there are always alternative correct descriptions of any situation: descriptions are inexhaustible.[1] Treating legal (or religious or sociological or 'common sense') descriptions as privileged represents a (covert) choice and not a datum. Such choices of terminology bring in more than 'mere description'. Further, outside a particular framework – the very one we are considering, which seeks to separate descriptive from ethical uses of language – we have no general reasons for thinking that a term which is used to describe cannot also and simultaneously be used to take up an ethical position. Rather, there is a 'natural process of give and take between the vocabulary we use for prediction and the vocabulary we use for control' (Rorty, 1983, p. 164). In adopting certain categories for social inquiry we also adopt a certain view of the social world, of its problem areas and of its fixed points, of the actions it makes available and ways in which their results are constrained. Within this view some ethical problems are salient and others invisible. Anyone who looked at the same domain of life through other lenses – perhaps taking seriously the perspectives of those who reject national and market economic categories, seeing their legal embodiment as injustice – may see other ethical problems and other constraints on their solutions.

From a utilitarian perspective it cannot be an ethically neutral matter to spread the categories and outlook of social science. Such activity would certainly *transform* consciousness; but might not *raise* it. It may, for all we know, *lower* consciousness, as Hampshire suggests. Only if utilitarian thinking could provide reasons for spreading one rather than another group of social and ethical categories would it be reasonable to make utilitarian deliberation more widely accessible by spreading a common set of categories which can then underpin widely accessible instrumental reasoning.

How could utilitarian thinking demonstrate the superiority of some grid of categories? Such a demonstration would have to reckon the results of using each possible grid of categories, and calculate and compare their benefits. However, this demonstration will be inaccessible to many unless social and economic categories are *already* generally shared, and will be indeterminate unless certain categories are *presupposed* in the reasoning which is to justify one rather than another conceptual grid. If so a choice among ways of looking at problems of development and world hunger cannot be given a fully utilitarian justification.

The difficulties which arise for utilitarian thinking about large-scale problems arise not only from beginning with a subjective theory of value and motivation, but also from requiring that the benefit of *all* available acts and policies be compared. Such comparisons demand not just some local and limited knowledge of likely results of action (any ethical theory will demand this much), but a comprehensive understanding of causes, so that the full range of options can be evaluated. The ambitions that end by generating an undischargeable 'overload' of obligations, begin in the claim that there is an algorithm for ranking all actions and policies in terms of their global results.

Just as 'humane' utilitarians shrink from literal calculation of benefit, so many of them shrink from the rigours of comparing all available actions. Many short cuts are proposed: utilitarians should rely on rules of thumb; they should choose the first satisfactory alternative, rather than seeking to optimize, and so on. However, such short cuts can destroy the appeal of utilitarian reasoning about distant hunger because they return it to some limited legal and social context, whose agents and agencies may rely on a cognitive structure that is blind to crucial problems, and complacent about their remedy. Contextual utilitarianism is not enough: 'starvation deaths can reflect legality with a vengeance' (Sen, 1981, p. 166).

These are not reasons for thinking that we are always unable to agree on descriptions of situations or that we entirely lack causal knowledge. None of the arguments advanced here assumes any form of relativism. They assume only that we lack nontrivial, ethically neutral descriptions of social situations that are accessible to all, and causal knowledge about global social and economic development which is neutral between various ethical positions. Hence practical reasoning which purportedly relies on ethically neutral descriptions and comprehensive instrumental calculation cannot be taken at face value. We presumably have widely accessible descriptions of social relations and considerable knowledge of the causal connections between both natural and social events, which can be used in deliberation. What we need are forms of ethical reasoning whose cognitive demands do not standardly exceed what is available to us, and which can criticize the empirical and causal claims on which they rely without once again assuming value-neutral social descriptions and causal knowledge.

Before we turn to look in other directions for such forms of ethical reasoning, we might ask whether a more limited utilitarianism could avoid some of these difficulties. Utilitarianism offers a comprehensive ethical theory. A lot would be achieved in ethical deliberation about problems of hunger and poverty even if we had only a theory of justice. Since famine and hunger in the modern world are mainly problems of the public domain, it may be enough to have a theory of global justice, and to do without any comprehensive ethical theory. If utilitarian difficulties arise from its ambitious attempt to provide a complete ethical algorithm, which needs a complete and neutral form of instrumental reasoning, then a more limited project might have greater success.

5   Beneficence, and Then Justice

Justice is traditionally thought to be independent of results. The slogan 'let justice be done though the heavens fall' puts the point hyperbolically. Justice is taken to differ from other ethical requirements because its standards must be met even when the results are less good over-all than those that might be achieved by breach of justice. Certain rules or standards or rights – rather than results – provide the form of justice. Hence deliberations about justice must look at what is done, or might be done, and not just at results.

This view of justice, and of conflicts between rules of justice and calculations of results, is as it stands too abstract for use. Before we can start talking about action, we need to understand the principles by which actions are to be specified and individuated. *One* way to pick out acts or policies is in terms of the results that they produce or are likely to produce. Utilitarian reasoning claims to be able to do just this. Far from being unconcerned about justice, utilitarians claim to capture everything that is important about it, and to offer a critical theory of justice. They see the rules of justice simply as those rules of action whose breach is likely to have the worst results. Mill (1861, pp. 310–311 and 320–332) put the matter quite firmly when he stated that

> if justice be totally independent of utility, and be a standard *per se*, which the mind can recognise by simple introspection of itself; it is hard to understand why that internal oracle is so ambiguous, and why so many things appear either just or unjust, according to the light in which they are regarded

and insisted that for an account of justice that was not hostage to established preconceptions it was necessary to recognize that justice is a name for certain moral requirements, which, regarded collectively, stand higher in the scale of social utility, and are therefore of more paramount obligation than any others; though particular cases may occur in which some other social duty is so important, as to overrule any one of the maxims of justice. Thus, to save a life, it may not only be allowable, but a duty, to steal, or take by force, the necessary food or medicine or to kidnap and compel to officiate the only qualified medical practitioner.

Utilitarian thinking can incorporate an account of justice; it can latch on to the traditional moral distinction between perfect duties (of justice), to whose performance particular others have a right, and imperfect duties to whose performance no other has any right. It does not have to accept or endorse established and conventional conceptions of the requirements of justice, but can criticize these by the yardstick of the more fundamental Principle of Utility. In this picture justice too is a matter of results. Rules of justice are discovered by calculating which actions are usually most important for securing good results. These rules may therefore be quite local and context bound; but their justification should be accessible wherever the Principle of Utility is accessible. Since the rules have a derivative status, exceptions to 'maxims of justice' in special circumstances are to be expected.

Objections to utilitarian justice mostly question its tendency to absorb problems of fair distribution into the pursuit of optimal results. This is a particularly serious difficulty in deliberation about acute hunger and poverty, since needs count for utilitarians only when reflected in preferences. Utilitarians may achieve sensitivity to justice only by defecting from the central utilitarian vision. Classical, maximizing utilitarianism may demand palpably unfair distribution; sophisticated utilitarianism that uses distribution-sensitive ranking principles concedes that benefit is not of overriding and unique moral importance.

Even if the traditional objections to utilitarian justice could be satisfactorily laid to rest by relying on some amended, distribution-sensitive ranking principle, the problems discussed in the last section will affect utilitarian thinking about justice. In utilitarian thinking, matters of justice are fully integrated in the net of consequential calculation. Justice is not a matter to which results are irrelevant, but simply the core of beneficence. In this framework appeals to justice do not escape the difficulty that they must rest on appeals to the supposedly value-neutral and comprehensive generalizations of social science. On the contrary, matters of justice are 'of more paramount obligation' precisely because they are concerned with the structure and administration of the public domain, which affects the happiness or misery of more individuals than do most other matters. What constitutes justice towards the Third World will depend upon ranking the likely results of all possible sets of rules for ordering economic and political affairs. If social scientists cannot provide global generalizations by which to rank the results of alternative possible conceptions of justice, or if the generalizations they provide use categories that are not ethically neutral, then utilitarian determinations of justice cannot be immune from the difficulties which affect utilitarian deliberations more generally. By integrating concern for justice into subjective, result-oriented thinking, utilitarian deliberation makes justice nothing other than basic beneficence.

Utilitarian reasoning does not, as is sometimes said, lack a theory of justice. It provides a clearer account of justice than some alternative starting points. Its difficulty is that the theory so grounded depends on an account of social science which is either resolutely bounded by currently established categories, so uncritical of them, or defiantly oblivious of those categories, so inaccessible to actual agents and agencies of social change. The same dilemma arises for utilitarian attempts to judge the justice of alternative development policies, or of proposed systems of property laws or proposed ways of restructuring the international order. Proposals that reflect currently established conceptions of justice are indeed accessible to some (but not to all) agents and agencies, but they are likely to introduce established and nonutilitarian categories of thought and are unlikely to produce optimal results; they provide no basis for questioning established social and economic categories and assumptions. Proposals that disregard the idioms of current institutional or individual discourse may be optimal in the abstract, but are for that reason unlikely to be accessible to the very agents and agencies whose action would be needed to institute the proposals.

Justice to the Third World cannot then be determined by the *explicit* structure of utilitarian reasoning. Such reasoning depends on *implicit* ethical commitments of various social and economic perspectives. It is these tacit commitments that make some ethical problems salient and submerge others, and which lead social 'scientists' to study some phenomena and relations but to neglect others. It is these commitments that confront utilitarian deliberators with the dilemma between reasoning in ways that are inaccessible because they are too abstract, or in ways that are inaccessible because they rely on some local idiom. More widely accessible deliberations would need a framework which allows general and critical discussion of alternative social and economic categories and perspectives. Even if utilitarian reasoning can be used at specific junctures in discussions of justice to the Third World, it provides an incomplete framework for such discussion.

Note

1   The phrase is Hampshire's. Descriptions of natural events are also multiple and reflect certain theoretical and perhaps even ethical commitments. These claims are made here for social descriptions only, merely because these concern consequentialist deliberators more (cf. O'Neill, 1984b).

6

The Rights of the Poor

> It is paradoxical, but hardly surprising that the right to food has been endorsed more often and with greater unanimity and urgency than most other human rights, while at the same time being violated more comprehensively and systematically than . . . any other right. (Alston, 1984, p. 9)

> Any system of property, national or international, is an institution with moral characteristics: claims of right or entitlement, claims about what is ours to use as we wish, carry only as much weight as the legitimacy of the institution will bear. (Nagel, 1977, p. 57)

1 Results and Acts

Serious practical deliberation about famine and world hunger has to think about the results which acts or policies may produce. When so much hangs in the balance for so many it would be frivolous to depend on ways of reasoning which are not at all concerned with results. Consequentialist ways of reasoning, which hinge everything on results, therefore seemed promising for deliberating about world hunger.

These merits are striking when consequentialism, and in particular utilitarianism, is considered in the abstract, but they shrink when we try to deliberate about actual situations. In consequentialist thinking descriptions of situations, lists of available actions, and even the reckoning of their consequences and calculation of their relative benefits, is not only difficult but readily assimilated to the categories, assumptions and working practices of existing institutions and their staff, or to received opinion about results and benefits. As a result consequential deliberation does not offer a tough-minded selection of optimal lines of action, but a pliable container into which established assumptions, preferences and ways of thought can be fitted. The abstraction of utilitarian theory may be a *theoretical* liability, but it is also the secret source of its *worldly* success. It provides a mode of deliberation plastic enough to accommodate received views, yet able to lend them the authority of high ethical theory. If utilitarian thinking were less accommodating it would be too abstract to guide action unless coupled with a scientific and comprehensive comparison of the perspectives of all possible institutions and ideologies. If we cannot adopt the abstracted and neutral standpoint of an ideal moral spectator or utilitarian legislator, or rely on expert social scientists or policy makers whose vision approaches theirs, these comparisons cannot be made. Nor is it possible to reshape utilitarian ways of thought so that they at least discriminate the core requirements of justice. In utilitarian thinking justice is a part of beneficence, and indeterminate unless utilitarian deliberation in general can be made determinate.

Fortunately, we do not have to focus all attention on results just because results are important. Results can often be achieved by insisting that acts are done or procedures followed, just as processes and action may sometimes be best ensured by demanding results. Legal systems, economic and political institutions and social practices and procedures of all sorts tend to produce certain sorts of results reliably, although they standardly operate by mandating or forbidding or permitting action of various sorts. Consequentialist deliberation would be inadequate if it merely identified optimal outcomes; it has also to identify the patterns of action and of regulation most likely to produce them. Equally, the action and policies which action-centred reasoning requires, permits or forbids may reliably produce certain results. There is no general reason for thinking that reasoning about action cannot secure results by guiding action.

However, action-centred ethical reasoning, on the face of it, is just as likely to become hostage to established and establishment modes of discourse as consequential reasoning. For actions must be individuated under some description or another, and these descriptions will be inaccessible unless they use categories available in established ways of thought. Very few of those who explore action-centred ethical reasoning think that there is any neutral standpoint from which actions and policies could be authoritatively and uncontroversially described and individuated (but see Steiner, 1974–75, pp. 44 ff.). On the other hand, action-centred ethical reasoning offers a framework of thought in which the demands of justice are standardly separated from other ethical demands and for this reason may prove more useful for ethical deliberation about public affairs. Faced with the enormous difficulty of finding a form of utilitarian deliberation which is neither abstract and inaccessible, nor uncritically and pliantly receptive of established positions, we have good reason to look in other directions.

2 Obligation, Right and Rights in the Abstract

We shall, in fact, have to look in *two* directions. Action-centred ethical reasoning is commonly conducted in either of two idioms. Traditionally, discussions of obligation and of right have been closely related. If we consider the matter sufficiently abstractly, there is no difference between a principle of obligation and a principle of right. Whenever it is right either for some assignable individual, A, or for unspecified others, to have some action, x, done or omitted by B, then it is obligatory for B to do or to omit x either for A or for unspecified others. One and the same principle defines what is right for A (or for unspecified others) to receive from B, and what it is obligatory (indeed right) for B to do for A (or for unspecified others). Indeed, in many European languages the same word is used to express the notions of right and of obligation; the terms *droit* and *Recht*, for example, can serve as translation for either. At this level of abstraction the only difference between the idioms appears to be that the notion of obligation looks at an ethical relationship from the perspective of agency and the notion of right looks at the same relationship from the perspective of recipience.

This correlativity between principles of right and of obligation is by far the most fundamental structural feature of action-centred ethical reasoning. Without correlativity, discourse about what is owed to some cannot show that action ought to be taken, and discourse about what is owed by some cannot show that anyone (specified or unspecified) has been wronged if nothing is done.

At a less abstract level, it soon emerges, it matters a lot whether discussion is conducted in the idiom of right or of obligation. It may be initially puzzling that there should be any important differences between a perspective that looks first at what treatment ought to be received from others and a perspective which begins with consideration of what ought to be done or forborne with respect to others. If correlativity holds, this is surely a trivial choice between equivalent vocabularies. The significance of the choice emerges when we consider a shift that can only be made within discussions that take the notion of right as primary. This is the shift from debate about *right action* to discussion of *rights*.

So long as we talk about what it is right for some agent or agency to do, we need not distinguish what is owed to specified others, and what is owed indeed, but not to specified others. Once we start talking about *rights* we assume a framework in which performance of obligations can be claimed. Holders of rights can press their claims only when the obligations to meet these claims have been allocated to specified bearers of obligations. In rights-based reasoning, rights can either be claimed of *all* others (here the obligation is *universal*, such as an obligation not to injure) or of some *specified* others (here the obligation is *special*, such as a worker's right to receive agreed payment from an employer). However, action which cannot be performed for all, nor is based on any special relationship, is unallocated so cannot be claimed: for it is not specified against whom the claim should be lodged. Reasoning which begins with the notion of rights cannot take account of obligations which are neither universal nor special, where no connection is made between specified bearers of obligations and specified holders of rights. Since the discourse of rights assumes that obligations are owed to *specified* others, *unallocated* right action, which is owed to unspecified others, tends to drop out of sight. Beyond the most abstract level of action-centred reasoning, a gap opens between obligations and rights. This gap makes a very great difference to action-centred reasoning about hunger and poverty.

3 Justice, and Then Beneficence

The shift from discussing *right* to discussing *rights* deflects attention from obligations to which no right corresponds. When obligations are unallocated, it is indeed right that those obligations should be met; but nobody has a right – an enforceable and waivable right – to the obligation being met (Feinberg, 1979, p. 144; Martin and Nickel, 1980, p. 166). In discussions of rights it is standardly claimed that requirements to help or benefit are not owed by specified bearers of obligations to specified claimants, and so that no right corresponds to such obligations.

Such obligations are then standardly seen as less imporant than those 'perfect' obligations whose performance can be claimed by right-holders. Hence there is a temptation to 'promote' certain obligations by insisting that there are corresponding rights, even if the supposed claimants of the 'right' find nobody who bears the counterpart obligation. When 'rights' are promulgated without allocation to obligation-bearers they amount to empty 'manifesto' rights, whose fulfilment cannot be claimed from others (Feinberg, 1979, p. 153).

A shift from discussion of right action to discussion of rights has evident advantages. It moves away from the most abstract level of ethical discussion, towards one which can be institutionalized and made accessible to actual agents and agencies. A list of universal rights might provide a grid of categories which make certain problems salient and show who ought to act to remedy them. If, for example, we could establish that there is a universal right to food, each hungry person would have legitimate claims against specifiable others. However, unless the obligation to provide food to each claimant is actually allocated to specified agents and agencies, this 'right' will provide meagre pickings. The hungry *know* that they have a problem. What would change their prospects would be to know that it was others' problem too, and that specified others have an obligation to provide them with food. Unless obligations to feed the hungry are a matter of allocated justice rather than indeterminate beneficence, a so-called 'right to food', and the other 'rights' of the poor, will be only 'manifesto' rights (Alston and Tomasevski, 1984).

The shift from discussion of right to discussion of rights adopts not merely the passive perspective of the *recipient* of action, but specifically the narrower perspective of the *claimant* of others' action. Rights discourse focuses on what ought to be done for legitimate claimants. Only failure to comply with universal obligations (owed to all others) or with special obligations (owed to others because of some special relationship) can violate rights. No agent or agency can have obligations to provide services, help and benefits for all others. Nobody can feed all the hungry, so the obligation to feed the hungry cannot be a universal obligation, and most of those who are hungry have no special relationship in virtue of which others should feed them, so special obligations will not be enough to remedy poverty and hunger (Goodin, 1985). Hence it seems that obligations to provide food, or other material needs and services, can *at best* have subordinate status in ethical deliberation in which the notion of rights is fundamental. This is the heaviest cost of the shift to the discourse of rights.

When those who take a rights approach to ethical reasoning distinguish between *narrow* or *perfect* obligations and duties and *wide* or *imperfect* obligations or duties, their interpretation of the distinction is firmer and harsher than that used by utilitarians in distinguishing justice from the rest of beneficence. Perfect obligations are taken to be those which can be *claimed* as a right; imperfect obligations are not owed to specified others, hence there is nobody who has a right to their performance. From the perspective of the claimant, which is central to theories of rights, imperfect duties offer little. Their performance can neither be claimed nor waived, and is not required by justice but is a matter of charity or optional beneficence.

A world in which rights discourse is thought the appropriate idiom for ethical deliberation is one in which a powerful theoretical wedge is driven between questions of justice and matters of help and benefit. Justice is seen as consisting of assignable, claimable, and enforceable rights, which only the claimant can waive. Beneficence is seen as unassignable, unclaimable and unenforceable. This theoretical wedge is reflected in many contemporary institutional structures and ways of thought. Legal and economic forms are seen as the limits of justice; voluntary, charitable and interpersonal activities are seen as the domain of beneficence. Once the discourse of rights is established, generosity, beneficence and help are likely to seem less important, especially in public affairs. Others' needs, even their extreme poverty, will only be thought of as injustice if they have special rights to have their material needs met. Since beneficence is only an imperfect obligation we may bestow it as we will. If we lavish our attention and help on those who already have enough, or on our own families, that will count as beneficence. In discussions of rights, mere need carries no independent weight.

This downgrading of beneficence casts doubt on the merits of approaching problems of hunger and destitution in terms of rights. If only matters of justice, whose omission would be an assignable wrong, can be claimed, then any rights-based approach to matters of famine and world hunger faces a sharp dilemma. *Either* action which might remedy or avert world hunger must be shown to be a matter of justice and so claimable and enforceable. *Or* it must be seen as 'only' a matter of beneficence, neither claimable nor enforceable, nor a matter for public action. If beneficence is seen as less than obligatory, perhaps only a matter of individual preference or style, it cannot remedy grave public problems. Those who rely on it will relegate global famine and destitution to the withering inadequacy of optional private charity (Nagel, 1977).

However, deliberation in which *obligations* rather than rights are taken as fundamental would not need to draw so sharp a distinction between obligations with and without assignable bearers and claimants. If obligations were fundamental, remedies and approaches to world hunger and destitution might be required partly by justice and partly by beneficence, and neither would depend on preferences or be optional. Here imperfect obligations remain obligations. Since a rights-based approach to hunger and poverty has the self-imposed disadvantage of taking beneficence much less seriously than justice, there must be other reasons behind its great predominance and success in contemporary deliberations about famine and world hunger, and many other problems of the public domain. These reasons are partly historical and partly conceptual; a short consideration of each can show a good deal about the strengths and difficulties of contemporary discussions of rights.

4   The Human Rights Movement

The prominence given to rights in some recent discussions of aid, development and famine was in part a response to the commitment of President Carter's administration to secure 'human rights' in other countries. This commitment made ethical deliberation conducted in terms of rights more readily accessible to some policy makers and administrators. It was a powerful reason for pursuing rights-based arguments about aid and development policy.

However, the commitment of President Carter's administration to 'human rights' itself reflected a longer tradition of ethical debate. International debates since the Second World War have relied heavily on the (sometimes ambiguous) discourse of rights. The United Nations committed itself to several declarations and conventions on human rights, in particular to the 1948 Universal Declaration of Human Rights, whose Article 25 conferred 'a right to a standard of living adequate for the health and well being of himself and of his family, including food'. The European Convention on Human Rights was promulgated in 1950, the Helsinki Declaration in 1975. A multi-faceted Human Rights Movement, involving many international and voluntary organizations, now aims to monitor violations of 'human rights' and to secure respect for them.

Behind this movement lies the authority of the grand eighteenth-century claims about the rights of man, including the US *Declaration of Rights*, the French *Declaration of the Rights of Man and of Citizen* and Tom Paine's *The Rights of Man*. However, this movement has no longer history. Discussions of obligation and justice, of beneficence and virtue, have been a staple of the most abstract and the most daily ethical discussions since antiquity; but discussion of rights was an eighteenth-century innovation. This is surprising if rights are as fundamental for ethical deliberation as is now often claimed.

It is also surprising that there is no corresponding attention to human obligations. Although serious writing on human rights acknowledges that any right must entail correlative obligations, we find no Universal Declaration of Human Duties, and no international Human Obligations Movement.[1] This suggests that the discourse of rights must have advantages that the discourse of obligation lacks.

This advantage is not that rights-based deliberation can guide action better. If appeal to some right can show a certain action to be required or forbidden, the same conclusion could be reached by appeal to the correlative obligation; indeed, obligation-based reasoning is *more* able to guide action since it allows for imperfect obligations without corresponding rights. Neither approach can guide action with the same precision as consequentialist reasoning purportedly can, since neither offers an algorithm for identifying an optimal action for each context. Either approach can detect ranges of problems, discern whose problems they are and which actions, policies or omissions would violate or fulfil rights or obligation. Both patterns of reasoning can be used to show certain actions or policies forbidden, others obligatory and yet others (merely) permissible. (Since the proposed patterns of reasoning are not algorithmic, they may be unable to show which of two or more incompatible obligations is more important.)

The present predominance of rights-based reasoning is therefore both novel and puzzling. It has various sources, some historical and others political and conceptual. One source is that reasoning about obligations with correlative rights, unlike reasoning about obligations without correlative rights, is well entrenched in institutional, and especially legal, contexts. However, appeals to human or natural rights are in many ways unlike appeals to institutional or legal rights.

Actual legal deliberation often centres on claims that some act or omission constitutes fulfilment or violation of an obligation or right. It appeals to statutory and other principles and precedents, and is evidently circumscribed by established regulations and categories. However, claims that 'human' or 'natural' rights are being violated are not claims that specified governments or institutions are failing in their prescribed obligations, or even in the obligations that international documents assign them. They are appeals that aim beyond established institutional and political frameworks, or customary rights and obligations. That they do so was, after all the essence of Burke's complaint against Paine, and of Paine's appeal to mankind. Those who complain that their rights have not been respected do not approach the established order as humble *petitioners*, but as wronged *claimants*. Their address is not that of loyal subjects, but of rational would-be citizens. The political power of appeal to human rights lies in its insistence that locally and legally established rights and obligations are no final court of appeal, and in its ostensible appeal to universal principles by which partial or inadequate concepts of justice may be judged and condemned.

When rights are written into legislation or institutional charters, or embodied in social practices, they become a standard to which appeal can be made, and which can be enforced within some jurisdiction. However, such institutional rights can be enforced precisely because they are *statutory* or *customary* rights, whose correlative obligations have been located within an institutional structure.[2] Arguments about the nature and scope of such rights can be settled by appeal to constitutions, charters and laws and social practices, but the *underlying* debates of the Human Rights Movement, as well as older debates about natural or moral rights, do not appeal to institutional rights at all, but rather to fundamental ethical standards which are said to constitute 'moral' or 'ethical' or 'natural' rights and to provide standards for judging and improving institutionalized rights. This is the basis of the claim that institutional rights and obligations themselves should be judged in terms of natural rights.

However, an ethical vindication or criticism of institutional rights *need* not appeal to natural or human rights at all. For example, if we could show that obligations to feed the hungry are ethically fundamental, the institutional structures by which they were secured would simultaneously secure some statutory rights to food (see Sen, 1984; Shue, 1984). Or if consequential reasoning showed that public provision of food was of great benefit, the institutions and practices which achieve it would also institutionalize rights to food. To show that rights are the *fundamental* ethical category we need deeper reasons than the fact that they provide *one* ethical basis for institutional rights. Other starting points would provide as firm an ethical basis for these.

5   Grasping Rights and Population Problems

Appeals to fundamental natural or human rights will only work if there are justifiable universal standards, which are generally, or at least very widely, accessible to agents and agencies with heterogeneous 'normal' ethical and political discourse. In the eighteenth century, appeal to the 'self-evidence' of certain rights was sometimes thought justification enough, which it clearly is not. Recent and more brazen writers have posited or postulated rights whose justification they could not discover. This method has, as Russell remarked in another context, all the advantages of theft over honest toil.

Those who do not shirk the toil most often appeal to the thought that all rights are fundamentally justified as rights to liberty, to which all men (more recently women) are entitled, and which is the only condition under which full human autonomy can be respected and flourish. As a justification of natural or human rights this thought is familiar but opaque. It suggests that particular claims about what rights there are can be settled by seeing which possible rights can consistently be held by all human beings and so constitute human liberty. If there are many consistent sets of possible rights, the largest of these will be the fullest realization of human liberty. It is by individuating distinct aspects of liberty that fundamental rights are established.

This suggests that rights discourse will be accessible to all only if some concept of liberty is universally accessible and universally accepted as the most basic ethical notion. Without such fundamental agreement, appeals to supposed components or aspects of liberty cannot regulate a universally accessible discourse about human rights. Appeals to liberty, particularly when given an indeterminate and abstract interpretation, do often engage a wide audience, but this wide appeal may rest more on shared rhetoric and vocabulary than on shared understanding. The great disagreements about which fundamental human or natural rights there are suggest that more determinate interpretations of human liberty are *not* universally accessible.

Some liberal writers, in particular libertarians, take a solely 'negative' view of liberty as 'freedom from interference', and propose that the most vital human rights are rights to engage in activities such as thought, worship, speech, publication and association, and in economic activities such as buying, selling and contracting, without state or other interference. Others, including both liberals and democratic socialists, take a more 'positive' view of freedom as autonomy or 'freedom to undertake' and conclude that the most basic human rights must also secure whatever is needed for activity to be undertaken. Basic rights must then include rights to some *means* of life, including food; at least some must be *'welfare' rights* to have certain fundamental needs met, rather than *liberty rights* to act without outside interference.

Clearly, these two interpretations of freedom lead not only to *different* but to *incompatible* claims about what human rights there are. Libertarians sometimes enjoy pointing this out. If there are unrestricted economic rights to run life on commercial lines and accumulate private property, there cannot be *rights* to food or welfare; if there are rights to food or welfare or health care or employment there cannot be unrestricted *rights* to engage in commercial activity. The activities that are freely chosen may not produce and deliver goods that would meet everyone's needs. Market economies respond only to needs which are backed by purchasing power – hence not to the most serious needs. The ambiguous rhetoric of rights allows the partisans of various

accounts of human rights to share the slippery ground of international declarations and charters. It also leaves both Western and
Soviet commentators claiming in all seriousness that it is the other
side's practice that constitutes a standard affront to human rights
(Kamenka and Tay, 1978; Garvey, 1978, chs I and VI). Nowhere
are disputes over rival conceptions of rights more vivid than in
discussion of the rights of the poor and destitute of the world.

If human rights are *only* liberty rights – rights to engage in
activity of all sorts, provided only that others' like rights are
respected – they can include no rights to have the means of life
provided, since that would oblige others to engage in specific
sorts of activity and so infringe some liberty rights. Unrestricted
rights to appropriate and control resources standardly leave some
people unpropertied, poverty-stricken and powerless. Strong
individual property rights are compatible only with weak conceptions of rights to the means of life, as rights to strive – for income,
property or employment. However, striving may fail. If freedom
of economic action is taken as basic, rights to guaranteed
economic minima are impossible. In this perspective, providing
for others' needs is beneficent and goes beyond respect for rights.
All rights could be respected only by a policy of *laissez faire*,
which would interfere with nobody's activities. We have here the
roots of the view that no injustice is done if the hungry and
destitute are left to themselves, since justice demands no more
than respect for human (liberty) rights. More worrying still, we
have here a position that sees almost anything except commercial
involvement and private charity as unjust approaches to North–
South problems, which will violate some rights. Taxation for
welfare purposes *within* a nation state is accepted as just by all but
some libertarian liberals, provided that those who are taxed have
consented to the arrangement through political institutions, and
so are not coerced. Transnational taxation for similar purposes
will seem unjust to those who take liberty rights as ethically
fundamental, since there are no transnational institutions by
which consent can be given to significant transfers of resources
(Nagel, 1977, pp. 58–60).

When rights are seen as rights to noninterference there are
scanty ethical grounds for political action to help the poor. There
are no institutions through which consent to transnational action
can generally be secured. The possibilities are reduced to private

charity (whose ethical importance a rights approach fails to secure), private investment in transnational corporations (whose purpose is profit for investors), and whatever action the governments of developed countries may take in pursuit of their national interest. Charity is not enough to remedy world hunger and the activities of transnationals and national governments have objectives as likely to harm as to help the poor.

The principle of seeking like liberties for all not only provides slight basis for helping the poor; it has also led to endless disagreements about what human or natural rights there are. Several areas of disagreement about liberty rights are particularly important in North–South debates. Discussions of population policy and procreative rights provide one example of sustained disagreements among protagonists of liberty rights.

If liberty rights are fundamental for ethical deliberation, population policies will be unjust if they interfere with procreative rights. If there are unrestricted rights to form families and to reproduce, public action to reduce population growth cannot legitimately go beyond the provision of contraceptive information and services. Yet advocates of liberty rights are deeply divided about what procreative rights there are. After 20 years of close debate some rights theorists think that 'a woman's right to choose' includes a right to choose abortion, and others that the 'unborn child's right to life' precludes any right to choose abortion (Sumner, 1981). However, without a determinate list of human or natural rights, it is hard to see which population policies infringe human rights and which do not. Such unclarities about the limits of procreative rights obstruct reasoning about the justification of population policies. This is far from trivial, since available forms of contraception remain unreliable, unsuited to conditions of poverty or unavailable to the poor. The importance of these disagreements was manifest at the 1984 Conference on World Population in Mexico City at which the US Government based its withdrawal of funding for all family planning programmes which included provision for abortion on the view that human liberty rights include a foetal right not to be killed but do not include a maternal right to terminate pregnancy (*People*, 1984). Unless disagreements about procreative rights can be settled, theories of liberty rights cannot guide deliberation about population policies.

6   Grasping Rights and Compensatory Justice

Disagreements about which economic rights there are persist even among advocates of liberty rights. Various liberal writers have tried to show that justice to the poor demands more positive action, while holding on to the picture of human rights as liberty rights. Some of them try, with considerable ingenuity, to show that the poor have *special* rights against the rich.

Some have suggested that *laissez faire* is inadequate on liberal grounds, because the present plight of the underdeveloped world was in (large) part produced by the activity of the developed world. They often point to the legacy of a colonial past, in which Third-World economies were developed to the economic advantage of the imperial power. Profits made in the 'South' were often 'repatriated' rather than reinvested locally; colonial industrial development and trade were restricted. Development in the 'North' was based in part on colonial exploitation. However, when the individuals whose rights were violated in the colonial past, and those who violated them, are both long dead, and the relevant institutions often defunct, past exploitation provides a slender basis for claiming that some poor countries (or groups, or regions, or individuals) now have *special* rights against some richer nations or corporations. The actual pattern of colonial violations of economic rights is complex and obscure. In the heart of darkness everything is murky. Many former colonies were economically backward when colonized; some colonial administrations did a good deal to modernize and develop the infrastructure of their colonies; it is always uncertain what the present would have been had the past not been colonial. *If* the plight of the poor could be attributed to past damage by colonial powers, then those powers could hardly claim that a policy of *laissez faire* to the poor respected their rights, so was just. Rather justice would require some effort to compensate for past violations of liberty rights in former colonies. However, if we cannot tell how far the predicaments of the present were produced by ancient wrongs, nor do much to tell which of those now alive have been so harmed, and which of them have benefited from those past violations, claims for compensation will be indeterminate and hard to allocate and so provide no certain remedy to the neediest (O'Neill, 1975; Sher, 1981).

Another argument to show that the poor have special rights suggests that the developed world owes the Third World compensation not on grounds of ancient but of present wrong. The present world economic order, it is claimed, harms the most vulnerable countries, and so harms the poor. *Laissez faire* is a mockery in a world where the rich and powerful control the 'rules of the game', and in particular those of international financial and trading arrangements. The details of such charges are enormously intricate; but the outlines are simple. *Laissez faire* could respect rights only if there were not already massive involvement by the powerful in the affairs of the Third World, but in fact there is massive involvement. The activities of transnational corporations, the operation of trade barriers and of banking and credit institutions, and above all the financial regulation of the international monetary system by the IMF (Brandt, 1980, ch. 13), show that the developed world already determines the basic conditions of economic life for many poor countries and so restricts many possibilities of action for those countries and for their citizens and limits liberty for many. Any claim that justice in the actual circumstances of today could be met by policies of *laissez faire* is only hypocrisy.

Put in this rather general way this argument is impressive, but its detailed implications are hard to determine. It might be used to justify a policy of total *laissez faire*. Could not the developed world *stop* violating liberties of the poor and vulnerable by severing all ties with them? Interestingly, such proposals have come neither from liberals of the developed world (who are generally keen on beneficial as well as profitable involvement), nor from advocates of *laissez faire* (who are traditionally blind to systemic effects) but mainly from radical writers on Third-World problems who argue that the only way to economic advance is to put an end to the 'dependent development' which is all the present world economic order permits (Kitching, 1982). In this picture foreign 'aid' and investment capital can only lead to distorted and dependent sorts of development, which neglects the needs of the poor. Sometimes they harm the poor directly, by setting up manufacturing processes and standards (e.g. in asbestos and chemical processing) which richer countries have outlawed as dangerous (Shue, 1981), or by marketing goods that cannot safely be used in poor conditions (such as infant foods or complex pharmaceuticals). More generally, it is the opportunity cost of inappropriate development that harms the poor indirectly. Investment goes to urban rather than agricultural projects, to imports of capital-intensive and unnecessary technologies or of luxuries for local elites. The political pressures for inappropriate development include transnationals' search for profitable investment, the strategic use of some 'aid' funds by certain 'donor' nations and the professional predilections of development experts. They are also reinforced by political forces *within* many poor nations. One anthropologist (Mair, 1984, p. 6) reminds us that in the South,

> Economic is made in cities where bureaucrats and legislators are gathered and the resentment of wage earners at a rise in the cost of food is quickly felt.

It is not surprising that some commentators conclude that foreign aid and investment capital should be foregone. Autonomous economic development may be slower, but will at least not be shaped by outside financial and national interests.

From the perspective of the human rights movement, the merits of autonomous development strategies are unclear. Such approaches would alter the 'rules of the game' in ways that prevent transnational corporations, the international banking and development institutions and developed nations from having as direct an influence on the economic development of a region as they might otherwise have had. Hence these institutions may infringe the liberties of those in the South less; but they will still control the 'rules of the game' in many ways, and affect the possibilities of action for any developing economy that aims to export or trade. In addition, any new 'rules of the game' may aim only at *national* autonomy and so fail to help the poor or to secure them liberty of action, while serving the interests of national and local elites.

Other proposals for autonomous development stress not *national* but *local* autonomy. Nation states are not the unit of poverty or hunger or dependence. Only cooperative and participatory movements of the poor, where leadership is local and 'rules of the game' are determined by the poor themselves should be thought of as embodying the principle of autonomous development (Harrison, 1983). In theory, such institutions might respect the rights of each individual and association; in practice it is deeply controversial how the coordination needed for economic advance and other sorts of development can be achieved within local and participatory institutions. Development needs capital formation and investment; and neither is available in a very poor economy which eschews imported capital unless somebody is squeezed hard. Effective development strategies often *must* limit liberties. While the anarchist aspect of some pictures of autonomous development may appeal to supporters of liberty rights, the reality of effective development strategies may be far from their ideal of mutual noninterference.

7 Rights to Subsistence

Some other liberal critics of the existing international economic order have taken a broader line in attacking the justice of *laissez faire* approaches to the Third World (O'Neill, 1975; Gewirth, 1979; Shue, 1980; Alston and Tomasevski, 1984; and cf. O'Neill, 1985d). They challenge the importance of the distinction between liberty and 'welfare' rights, which most liberal thinking and some UN documents accept, and suggest that adequate respect for liberty rights themselves also demands respect for minimal economic and social claim rights. There is no adequate way to respect others' rights, including any rights to action, unless we also respect certain 'welfare' rights, including a right to minimal subsistence. Human rights are the conditions of human autonomy, or positive liberty. Hence *any* respect for rights needs some positive action, and not mere noninterference. For the vulnerable (see Shue, 1980, p. 19):

> The classic liberal's main prescription for the good life – do not interfere with thy neighbour – is the only poison they need.

What is needed, Shue argues, is a theory of *basic rights*, that is of those rights (whether 'welfare' or liberty rights) which cannot be sacrificed without defeating the exercise and enjoyment of all rights. These basic rights may not include all (mutually consistent) liberty rights, but do include 'welfare' rights to the provision of sufficient physical security and subsistence to make some action, hence some exercise of rights, possible. It is a sham to maintain that noninterference respects rights if it either denies or fails to secure for others even the minimum they need to exercise those rights. Rights, Shue suggests, are misperceived if thought of as sharply dividing into negative liberty rights (action rights), whose correlative duties demand only noninterference and positive 'welfare' rights (that is rights to receive, not positive rights in the sense in which statutory or customary rights are positive) whose correlative duties demand action and so restrict others' liberties. *No* right can be secured if others merely do not interfere, and the priority assigned to liberty rights in so much of the liberal tradition is illusory. Even the most basic liberty rights cannot be respected unless *action* is taken to set up institutions which secure them and to prevent or restrain institutions and individuals which threaten liberty. Respect for all rights requires positive action as well as negative noninterference (see Shue, 1980, p. 53):

> the common notion that *rights* can be divided into rights to forbearance (so-called negative rights), as if some rights have correlative duties only to avoid depriving, and rights to aid (so-called positive rights), as if some rights have correlative duties only to aid, is thoroughly misguided. This misdirected simplification is virtually ubiquitous among contemporary North Atlantic theorists and is, I think, all the more pernicious. . . . It is duties and not rights that can be divided among avoidance, aid and protection. And – this is what matters – every basic right entails duties of all three types . . .
> . . . the very most 'negative'-seeming right to liberty, for example, requires positive action by society to protect it and positive action by society to restore it when avoidance and protection both fail.

Shue's point is convincing and highly damaging to arguments which depend upon drawing a clear distinction between positive and negative rights. What he shows is that such a distinction works only at a very indeterminate and abstract level. Once we consider what it takes to set up institutions which secure any right, as we must if reasoning about rights is to be determinate enough to guide action, noninterference will not be enough.

There is no way in which 'doing nothing' can secure freedom from torture, any more than it can secure freedom from starvation.

However, Shue's position is also highly damaging to the most standard reasons given for taking the notion of a right as *fundamental* in ethical deliberation. The supposed grounding of human rights in the notion that they jointly constitute the largest consistent set of human liberties or human autonomy depends upon being able to determine whether proposed sets of rights are mutually consistent, and which set is maximal. As soon as we acknowledge that basic rights require action and not mere forbearance, this line of thought is blocked. Rights which require positive action by others will be in conflict in all sorts of circumstances. The chilling but popular image of a set of agents whose individual spheres of action bound and determine one another, and establish the maximal limit of liberty, is illusory. If the definition of spheres of 'self-regarding' action depends on others' intervention, boundaries are not and cannot be uniquely fixed.

There are various related reasons for doubting even that the libertarian liberal image of a 'most extensive liberty compatible with like liberty for all' provides a coherent starting point for ethical thinking (O'Neill, 1979). Even if we know how to determine which sets of possible liberty rights are consistent, we lack a way to gauge that one consistent set of liberty rights is 'larger' than others. If rights are individuated in terms of act descriptions, there can be no Pareto optimal set of rights and no metric of rights, any more than there can be a calculus of descriptions. We cannot tell whether a right to life is *larger* than a right to freedom of expression. Theories of rights which deny that there are welfare rights avoid *one* range of difficulties; but they cannot avoid the more serious difficulties that infect all theories of rights.

There is perhaps no reason why we should try to answer these arcane questions about human rights. However, if we do not we can no longer lean on the traditional claim that certain natural or human rights are basic because they constitute a part of the largest possible human liberty. Arguments to justify natural or moral rights will then have to rely on other foundations. This may prove hard, because the argument is about the *starting point* for ethical deliberation. If we were arguing for *institutional* rights, we might after all invoke another starting point. We might claim that enacting rights would produce desired results, or be a reasonable way in which to fulfil obligations. However, when we are trying to work out which natural or moral rights there are, we can hardly appeal to these rival starting points. If we were only considering which statutory rights should be secured, the importance of debating whether liberty and 'welfare' rights are fundamentally distinct would in any case fade. Nobody doubts that *institutional* rights may demand action as readily as forbearance, nor that ethical reasoning which does not begin by taking liberty rights as fundamental might show that action to institute and secure others' subsistence was more important than noninterference.

In discussion of North–South problems, theories of rights often seem to point to conclusions from which their very proponents shrink. Many writers hope that some modified or improved theory of rights will yield different results. Yet so far the most promising modification, which blurs the boundary between liberty and welfare rights, simultaneously erases the most promising foundation for any theory which makes rights ethically fundamental.

8 Human Rights and Political Change

In spite of their obscure foundations and ambiguous contents, theories of rights retain enormous appeal and resonance. This is surprising given the difficulty of making any rights theory which is determinate enough to guide action seem plausible. It may, perhaps, be due to the remarkable, but partial *accessibility* of incomplete and indeterminate theories of rights. Discourse about rights is highly *accessible* to those who believe themselves to hold certain rights, *even when it is unclear who holds the correlative obligations.*

Appeals to rights attract so much attention and support because they speak past existing institutions and invoke supposedly universal standards. Those who respond do not have to see themselves in terms imposed by the established social order. A demand that human rights be respected not merely criticizes the performance of established institutions and ways of life, but repudiates their labels. Those who claim their rights can see themselves in more abstract terms simply as human beings, so entitled to human rights. In certain contexts – but not in all – the rhetoric of rights may help empower the powerless.

However, rights-based reasoning pays a high price for its minimal accessibility. The shift from the perspective of the petitioner, who accepts the established order and his or her place in it, to that of the claimant, who disputes established power and its labels, can sometimes be an energizing and liberating transition, particularly for those who act to secure *others'* rights. However, it does not reject the passive perspective of recipience. A claimant is still somebody whose first demand is for *others'* action. There is a deep sense in which discourse about rights is not the discourse of active *citizens* but of *claimants* who aspire to receive whatever they may be entitled to. The appeal to rights becomes accessible across social, political and ideological boundaries by endorsing a picture of human beings not indeed as mere subjects, but still as passive claimants. An appeal to rights can be heard so widely because it depicts the holders of rights only under the most indeterminate descriptions, as abstract individuals with unspecified, unmet needs or desires or preferences and with unspecified plans and potential for action.

This result may seem the unavoidable corollary of insisting that practical, including ethical, deliberation be widely accessible. After all, any message which can reach others, without social, political or ideological restrictions, is going to have to rely on categories of discourse that are very widely shared. Looked at in this way the eighteenth-century rhetoric is abstract to good purpose. Since the audience was to be universal, the terms of discourse had to be so also. However, the most necessary audience for rights discourse is *not* the universal audience of right holders, but the audience of those whose action can institutionalize and secure respect for rights. No doubt that audience will be able to follow debates about human rights – abstraction guarantees that too – but they may not find the vocabulary of rights salient or that its message about what has to be done, and by whom, is either definite or convincing. Because it speaks first to those who claim their rights, and not to those who have the power to meet or spurn their obligations, rights discourse often carries only a vague message to those whose action is needed to secure respect for rights. Widepread acceptance of the abstract rhetoric of rights coexists with widespread failure to respect rights.

The remoteness of discussions of rights from effective action shows in their tendency to leave behind the vocabulary of action and to adopt a reifying vocabulary for individuating rights. We hear of rights to life, to liberty and to property; to freedom of conscience, of worship, of expression and of publication; to security, to nationality, to subsistence and specifically to food. This reifying vocabulary suggests (mis-leadingly) that there is some good which the holder of a right is entitled to hold or possess, as though all rights were a species of property right. It also obscures the underlying correlativity of rights and obligations. Reification is not an innocent manner of speaking. It is an idiom which makes it hard to see the connection between what some institutions, collectivities and individuals are entitled to and what others are obliged to do. It also makes it hard to see the connection between the very general rights claimed in the UN Charters and in other Declarations of Rights and various sets of prohibitions, obligations and regulations which might be proposed as ways to secure respect for those rights.

Discussions of rights only get down to business when they abandon reifying rhetoric and go back to the vocabulary of action. If, for example, we want to know what a right to life is, we must ask not 'What is life?' but rather 'Which sorts of obstructions or risks to life ought to be forbidden for all or for some agents and agencies, and which sorts of support for life ought to be required from which agents and agencies?' Debates about a 'right to life' only become serious, and acquire the potential for guiding action, when they become debates about counterpart obligations. The same holds for rights to food (Alston and Tomasevski, 1984) and even for property rights, where the reifying vocabulary is most nearly at home. To know whether a property right has been observed or violated we need to know which sorts of action various types of ownership preclude and require, both of owners and of various other agents and agencies. Ownership is a complex bundle of prohibitions and entitlements which secure a more-or-less exclusive use of various aspects of what is owned to specified agents or agencies. Only when we have got this far can we even begin to *ask* important questions such as whether either capitalist or socialist conceptions of property rights are ethically adequate. Similarly, with rights to food: it is no accident that the most serious recent discussions of such a right concentrate on delineating the corollary obligations (see Alston and Tomasevski, 1984, especially the paper by Shue).

When rights are individuated or grasped using a reifying vocabulary, discussion tends to remain at a high level of abstraction. This can help secure a *minimal* degree of communication across national and ideological boundaries. At the level of international charters the rhetoric of rights secures widespread agreement; but discourse about rights, whether reifying or not, also tends to *hamper* debate which is generally accessible. Rights can be promulgated, asserted and claimed even when the conceptual capacities and powers of action of those against whom the rights are held are inadequate to comprehend or to meet the requirements placed on them. Despite its supposed individualism, discourse about rights often makes do with a remarkably indeterminate view of agency.

In the end, action-based ethical deliberation can be accessible and action-guiding only if it talks about *action*. The vocabulary of rights has a complex formal structure, but is oddly remote from action, and from the established categories of many whose action might be needed. Any plausible way of specifying just which rights various agents and agencies may have, or whether they ought to be enforced or how they might be justified must lead back into discussion of action and of the powers and capacities of the agents and agencies whose action is needed. Ultimately, these discussions must raise fundamental *political* questions. In discussions of world hunger and poverty, appeals to rights *avoid* the question of agency. They do not ask how obligations which are neither universal nor special should be allocated. Although 'focusing on the right to food provides a rallying point around which to mobilise the starving masses' (Alston, 1984, p. 61), it may fail to mobilize those who have the power to change the lives of those masses (Hoffmann, 1981, p. 141):

> Human rights may be at the root of all social arrangements, but the politics of human rights is essentially a way of dealing with the surface of the problems caused by political regimes and economic systems, with symptoms rather than causes. When we examine the problems of distributive justice we reach the two fundamental questions of politics: Who commands? and Who benefits?

It is powerful agents and agencies who command and benefit; but the rhetoric of rights speaks mainly to the powerless. Rights discourse is at home and can guide action with precision when it invokes institutional rights, whose counterpart duties are allocated; it is dislocated outside established frameworks. It is therefore not an appropriate matrix for *fundamental* ethical and political debate. A claim that the developed world, or a transnational corporation, or local landlords violate rights to life, food or subsistence in parts of the Third World may sound impressive. Since it speaks most forcefully to suffering claimants, the message may be inaccessible or half heard by those with power to bring change. Bentham was right when he observed that 'a *declaration of rights* would be but a *lop-sided job* without a *declaration of duties*' (Bentham, n.d., p. 526).

Notes

1   In older writings it was common enough to take notions of obligation and duty as fundamental. In modern times Simone Weil subtitled her work on human obligations only 'Prelude to a Declaration of Duties towards Mankind' (Weil, 1949). Some recent work on the notion of a right to food is moving increasingly to discussion of the counterpart, allocated obligations (Shue, 1980, 1984; Alston and Tomasevski, 1984); but the shift reflects a focus on enforcing or institutionalizing rights rather than a shift of ethical foundations.

2   Institutional rights and obligations are traditionally referred to as 'positive' rights and obligations, and contrasted with 'natural' or 'human' (or 'fundamental' or 'background', Dworkin, 1977; Sen, 1984) rights and obligations. I have used the term 'institutional' rather than 'positive' to avoid confusion with rights that are said to be 'positive' as opposed to 'negative', in that they demand others' action and not merely their noninterference.

7
Obligation and Need

> The notion of obligations comes before that of rights, which
> is subordinate and relative to the former. A right is not
> effectual by itself but only in relation to the obligation to
> which it corresponds, the effective exercise of a right spring-
> ing not from the individual who possesses it, but from other
> men who consider themselves as being under a certain
> obligation towards him. (Weil, 1949, p. 3)

1 Categories of Obligation

For different reasons neither consequentialist nor rights-based
reasoning can guide deliberation about problems of famine and
world hunger in terms likely to be accessible to the agents and
agencies most able to act. A focus on obligations has the reputation
of being no less abstract than either of these; and unlike them is
not nowadays supposed to be fundamental in public life. It is,
however, the ubiquitous background idiom of much public and
private discussion and deeply embedded in the practices of daily
life as well as in the lives of many institutions. Courts and
policemen, schools and parents, governments and politicians,
banks and businessmen, and aid agencies and relief workers
constantly discuss who ought to do what, what to do if others fail
in their obligations, and occasionally, no doubt, how to evade
obligations they acknowledge. The language of obligation is a
traditional idiom of daily and of theoretical discussion of ethics
and politics. Its disadvantage may be not that it is unavoidably
abstract (and so too indeterminate to guide action), or inaccessible
to agents and agencies with the capacities and powers to make
changes, but that in the forms that are accessible it is readily
captured by established and establishment categories and assumptions about what problems there are and who ought to do what
about them. If so its accessibility would be quite restricted.

If the only obligations are those that institutions acquire from their charter, individuals from their social roles and collectivities from their traditions, then the language of obligation will always be conservative and local. Appeals to obligation will be accessible, indeed they may be very effective, but will not criticize the institutions or roles that generate those obligations. The boundaries between different 'spheres of justice' and the constitution of each would be beyond ethical criticism (Bradley, 1876; Walzer, 1981, 1983, chs 2 and 3).

The implications of such views of the obligations of distributive justice for the poor of the world are plain. Where the boundaries of different spheres of life are already set, and maintained by powerful forces, there will be no sphere of life which generates obligations to change or to challenge the current 'rules of the game'. There will, for example, be no way to challenge the rules by which landlords in Bangladesh follow law and custom in extracting money from their tenants; no way in which to challenge established fiscal rules and banking practices by which poor countries find the terms on which they receive 'aid' can later cost a crippling proportion of annual revenue in debt repayment; no way to challenge agribusiness investment even when it replaces subsistence with cash crop farming and increases dependence on imported and expensive grain (Dinham and Hines, 1983).

This conception of obligation as local has been challenged since antiquity. Theories of justice, from Plato to John Rawls, insist that at least some features of justice do not vary with tribe or city or state or ethnic background. Obligations of beneficence too have long been thought to stretch beyond boundaries. In Christian thinking the *neighbours* whom we should help are not confined within the same ethnic or political boundaries. Some obligations are thought to bind across the firmest cultural and political boundaries, and to challenge the best established 'rules of the game'.

The appeal of such claims is obvious. If a theory of obligation can transcend local political and ideological frontiers, it may (like theories of natural or human rights) provide universal standards of right action. It would not approach these only by way of the recipients' perspective which theories of rights adopt, but could address the agents and agencies on whom obligations fell directly. It would really use the language of citizens and powerful agencies rather than the rancorous rhetoric of rights. Such reasoning might show certain agents or agencies both of the developed and of the undeveloped world what obligations world hunger and poverty place on them. It might sometimes be *useful* to restate the obligations of the rich and secure in terms of the claims of the poor and vulnerable, or to point to the benefits of obligatory action. Since these would be derivative claims, they would not rely fundamentally on ethical discourse that guides agents indirectly by reference to the rights of claimants or to the benefits of just action. Theories of obligation focus on actions themselves; they speak directly to those of whom they demand action.

However, direct speech is useless if it is inaudible. What is needed is a theory of obligation which is not only *universal and critical* but *accessible to the relevant agents and agencies*. Both consequentialist theories and theories of rights are most accessible to actual agents and agencies when they do not aim at universal (or even wide) scope, but embrace locally established and hence accessible categories and assumptions. However, they are best able to criticize locally established standards and categories and institutions when more abstractly stated – and so inaccessible for many agents. What reason is there to think that a theory of obligation (and specifically a theory of justice) can escape this dilemma and be both accessible and critical? Are not abstract theories bound to be inaccessible?

The problem could be put as follows: obligations to do or omit actions of various sorts are individuated by act descriptions. We might have obligations to act justly or generously, or more specifically to contribute to grain reserves or to tithe our incomes or not to collect debts from the poor.[1] Obligations are met when those who hold them act and forbear in ways specified by certain descriptions. Since descriptions are indeterminate, no obligation wholly specifies the ways in which it may be fulfilled. If the descriptions, whether relatively abstract or relatively determinate, are to be understood and judged pertinent by actual agents and agencies, they must be connected to agents' vocabulary of action. So if the vocabulary of action of different contexts varies greatly, how can there be universal or even widespread obligations? Even when the vocabulary of action of other societies and alien contexts is understood, it is often held to focus on insignificant aspects of action and to neglect vital ones. Understanding alien perspectives is not enough for practical purposes: their categories have also to seem appropriate and salient. Novels about colonial experience, from E. M. Forster's *A Passage to India* to Anthony Burgess' *Malayan Trilogy*, show how far – tragically and comically – views of a situation from distinct ideological perspectives can diverge. Where perceptions of action diverge radically, how can there be generally accessible reasoning about obligations? Is not such reasoning as unavoidably tied to local context as is accessible reasoning about results?

While an adequate and action-guiding account of obligation needs locally accessible and salient act-descriptions, it *also* needs more abstract act-descriptions. Even within a determinate social context, where obligations are well specified, transitions from more abstract to more determinate act descriptions are crucial for any process of practical deliberation. Simple deliberations such as 'We do not want to be without food, so we do not want to eat the grain too fast' moves from a rather abstract description – 'being without food' to a more determinate one – 'eating the grain too fast'. Any theory of obligation which can guide action, *even if only in local context*, has to provide for moves from more abstract to more specific descriptions of the problems and obligations of particular agents in contexts of action.

If all deliberation allows such transitions, however, may it not also lead *beyond* locally established views? There are always many determinate ways of enacting abstractly specified obligations. Some match locally established conceptions of what ought to be done; others do not. The most daily discussions of obligations often dispute whether an action described in specific ways can be seen as falling under other more abstract descriptions. This daily form of *specificatory reasoning* is a starting point for open-ended and ultimately for philosophical inquiry. It is the starting point also for Plato's *Republic*. Before ever Thrasymachus disrupts their conversation, Socrates and his friends ask in the daily idiom of Athens whether 'telling the truth and giving back what one owes' (*Republic*, pp. 321–322) are what it takes to give every man his due. They wonder whether returning a knife to its owner when he is in a frenzy could be required by justice. Does such a relatively determinate case fall under this more abstract principle of justice? To judge this they had to think more carefully about the principle itself; and that thinking proved both fundamental and political. It took them away from the locally established account of justice with which the *Republic* begins to a wholly revised understanding of what is due to each.

2   Problems, Principles and Deliberation

A theory of obligation cannot be critical of received accounts of the spheres of life and their obligations unless it includes a critical method for determining *which* problems are salient, *whose* problems they are and *which* actions are available. Only if we have a critical account of deliberation – of the specificatory reasoning by which a moral agenda can be established, debated and revised – can ethical reasoning avoid echoing locally received accounts of salient problems, their allocation and available action. Although such deliberation is the stuff of daily practical debate, both personal and institutional, it has recently had far too little explicit philosophical treatment.

One classical and deeply suggestive discussion of the topic is Kant's treatment of judgement.[2] Because situations and actions can be described in inexhaustibly many ways, *all* reasoning about action must move between different descriptions of situations and actions. It must work out *both* whether given, relatively abstract, descriptions of situations and principles of action would be satisfied by certain more determinate cases and decisions *and* whether given cases and acts which are seen as falling under rather specific descriptions would or would not (in a given context) also satisfy certain more abstract descriptions. Kant calls the former *determinant* and the latter *reflective* judgement. Neither sort of judgement follows an algorithmic procedure (Kant, 1781, p. A 134; Kant, 1790, pp. 179–181).

A given description or principle will be exemplified by many situations or acts whose more determinate descriptions vary. All application of principles or rules involves determinate judgement, for which complete rules cannot be given. Nor can a given act or situation which will fall under indefinitely many descriptions and principles be mechanically judged as of one or another type. Here 'reflective' judging is needed to find an appropriate more abstract description or principle (Kant, 1790, p. 179).

> If the universal (the rule, principle or law) is given then the judgment which subsumes the particular under it is determinant. . . . If however only the particular is given and the universal has to be found for it, then the judgment is simply reflective.

The transitions made in both *determinant* and *reflective* judging are not, however, random or unreasoned. A given problem or action can be defended as an appropriate instantiation of some more abstract principle – or rejected as inadequate. Acting justly to others cannot simply be equated with maintaining established laws, institutions and market structures. A principle of beneficence cannot simply be equated with a policy of giving to charity. Equally, more specific accounts of problems and actions cannot automatically be brought under more abstract ethical principles. Returning a knife to a man in a frenzy cannot easily be defended as merely one way of giving him his due. Nor can we just posit that a pattern of involvement with the poor which determines the framework of their economic life constitutes a policy of *laissez faire*. Nor can we take it for granted that giving trivial amounts of disposable income to voluntary relief agencies constitutes beneficence. Such claims are open to discussion and to rejection.

Both reflective and determinant judging standardly *begin* within locally established grids of categories. In trying, for example, to determine what would constitute beneficent action to others who are poorer and hungrier, we may *initially* be drawn towards standard and admired examples of good works. We might *start* by thinking about giving to voluntary agencies, or the more arduous giving of Mother Teresa or of Gandhi. In trying to think about what would constitute justice towards the very poor, we might *begin* by thinking of standards of commercial honesty or fair dealing which we respect in dealings nearer home. These may be moral starting points, but neither reflective nor determinant judging has to be limited by established ethical outlooks. Just as Socrates and his friends found themselves probing and questioning a view of justice that was established in Athens, so we can ask whether a proposed account of what it takes to live up to some abstract principle of justice or beneficence is adequate in a given context, and (if it is not) can hunt for a better account. The adequacy of descriptions of pressing problems, their allocation, and of available acts and policies, to more abstract principles is always open to further question, hence ultimately open to questions that reach beyond locally established categories and views.

In result-oriented thinking the only way to escape the hold of established and establishment ethical categories upon ethical deliberation appeared to lie in finding some value-neutral and scientific perspective on all the problems, possibilities and results of action in a given domain. Without 'neutral' and 'scientific' accounts of problems, policies, and results, calculations and ranking of benefits could not transcend local boundaries. Yet any social science whose categories were 'neutral' might not be widely accessible to actual agents and agencies. The possibility of critical ethical deliberation seemed to hinge on discovering a value-neutral social science and then imposing its grid of categories.

In action-oriented reasoning, critical deliberation can be understood in a less demanding way. Here we do not have to suppose that there is some Archimedean point, which affords the only correct perspective on all human predicaments and possibilities. We have only to assume that the agents and agencies in a particular context have a 'moral starting point' – the grid of categories of some outlook or milieu – which allows them to raise at least some questions whose answers may provide reasons for shifting the starting point. Any agents or agencies whose conceptual framework was wholly impervious to questioning and progressive emendation would indeed be locked into a conceptual grid from which other viewpoints were inaccessible. Actual agents and agencies, as opposed to idealized rational choosers and ideal-typical institutions and collectivities, unavoidably use conceptual grids that are open and porous to large ranges of questions and possibilities.

If the categories that form those grids are to be used in *any* form of practical deliberation – even the most local and contextual – they must be connectable both to more abstract and to more determinate categories. If, for example, we begin with some category such as 'helping our own in hard times' we will unavoidably find ourselves involved in debates about the connections between these categories and others. What exactly constitutes help? Who are 'our own'? Are they only kin? If so, how distant? What constitutes 'hard times'? Even where there is local agreement about paradigmatic cases of helping one's own, redescription of certain acts can often show them in a new light. Moral starting points can be changed. What used to seem required help for needy others, which could not be neglected by the rich without shame, now seems to many unrequired charity which goes beyond all duty. Cherished ideals such as large families, traditional ways of life, and motherhood as a vocation can and have been questioned. Such changes in established views may not all be improvements. They often reflect changes in the circumstances of life – help to strangers *must* take different forms in traditional and in mass societies. However, where we can find reasons for reviewing and revising the grid of categories with which we begin, we can also have reasons for thinking that some transformations of consciousness are reasoned, so raise and not merely change consciousness.

Action-centred reasoning *can* therefore move beyond locally established views. In all reasoning about action, agents and agencies have to judge (determinantly) what it will take to act on certain principles in that situation and (reflectively) which principles and descriptions certain problems, acts or policies exemplify. Individuals may ask what gratitude requires in a particular case; development workers or civil servants may ask whether handling a given case in terms of such and such a rule is compatible with their guidelines or mandate; executives may ask whether company policy could be interpreted in this or that other way; negotiators may ask whether some action by a foreign government should be seen under this or that description.

The *standard* modes of reasoning of all such agents and agencies depend on being able to shift between alternative descriptions of problems, actions and policies. Different agents and agencies may be able to shift more or less far in the ways in which they are able to construe or to reconstrue the problems and the possibilities that confront them. Many do not lose all grip on deliberation even when the shift is pretty radical, provided that it starts from a recognised point. When Christ suggested a radically revised answer to the question 'Who is my neighbour?' he silenced but did not lose his audience. We have clear historical examples of transformations of grids of categories, and of social and political movements which brought about transformations. An evident advantage of action-centred reasoning is that it is open to such transformations and that they may be achieved bit by bit. Here criticisms of received views do not depend on prior discovery of the complete results of alternative global development policies.

3   Principles of Obligation in the Abstract and in Context

However, critical patterns of deliberation about the specification of problems and actions are not enough for critical ethical reasoning about obligations. It is also essential to rely on a theory of obligation which is not itself hostage to whatever limited and context-bound principles of obligation agents and agencies may inherit as their 'moral starting points'. A critical theory of obligation which is neither inaccessible nor assimilated to received views must, like the theory of deliberation with which it is combined, both connect to and criticize the grids of categories with which actual agents and agencies are at home.

Many views of obligation fail in one or other respect. Some are evidently hostage to established and establishment views. They amount to a theoretical articulation of the practice and discourse of particular institutions and collectivities, and the social roles that they define. Such theories are unsuited to challenging or revising the demarcation of spheres of life, social roles and obligations which provides their own horizon. They are particularly ill-suited to handling global problems which involve many agents and agencies with divergent grids of categories. The moneylenders or landlords of an impoverished region may have an acute sense of their obligations – which requires them to persist in collecting debts and rent even when this will destroy lives and livelihoods. Such views of obligation are part and parcel of 'normal' ethical and political discourse, and unsuitable for assessing, defending or challenging received views, or the categories in which they are formulated.

Other theories of obligation are more distant from the standard practice and outlook of actual agents and agencies. Many rely on a theological framework, and include an account of the duties of man, or of various sorts and conditions of men and women, which is to some extent critical of current demarcations of spheres of life and their obligations. The suggestion that Jews should render unto Caesar what is Caesar's proposes a demarcation between political and economic life on the one hand and religious concern on the other, which has had perennial influence. Much could be different, not least in the impoverished South, if Christ's authority could not be invoked on behalf of a depoliticized Church. Such accounts of obligation show that a theory can be accessible to actual agents and agencies and yet to a considerable extent critical of current conceptions of ethical problems and obligations. Christian history is not entirely a history of an established Church buttressing established categories and received values. However, religious categories and conceptions of obligation may be alien and inaccessible beyond the pale of a religious community or church. A theological theory of obligation can be widely accessible – among the converted, and among those whose social institutions and practices and categories of thought bear the traces of past religious commitment. However, only those who accept a theology and its wider vision of the appropriate demarcation of spheres of life, social roles and obligations can use such theories to criticize current social and economic relationships.

The road from theological conceptions of obligation – which at least were potentially accessible to all the faithful – to more abstract conceptions, which aspire to yet wider accessibility, has beckoned since the eighteenth century. Yet the journey still proves troublesome. Secular ethics has explored various possibilities, but has often treated notions of obligation as ancillary to good results or to the securing of human rights. These approaches have perhaps been fruitful in handling many problems, but we have seen that they are of limited use when the problems are global and involve agents and agencies with diverse grids of categories, and discrepant conceptions of their 'normal' obligations. Reasoning about problems of world hunger and global economic and social development would go forward more easily in a framework which recognises the importance of shifting descriptions of actions, rather than relegating these shifts to an undiscussed framework of ethical deliberation.

However, there are well-known difficulties in finding an ethical theory in which reasoning about action (and so about obligation) is central, which is both generally accessible and yet able to criticize established ethical views. The popular image of Kant's ethics is a warning for anybody who tries to find a theory of obligation which is generally accessible, yet genuinely critical. Kantian ethics is widely admired for its lofty quest for the 'supreme principle of morality'. It is also widely rejected because it seems too abstract to guide action – unless covertly supplemented with views derived from established ethical positions. Hegel's criticism has the form of many: Kant was able to show theft forbidden on the assumption of property rights – but that showed nothing about property rights. Kant's ethic is also standardly charged with inability to address any but individual agents, and so with irrelevance to the deliberations of institutions and collectivities. Still worse, it appears to use an unconvincingly idealized conception of individual autonomy, and so to be irrelevant even in the deliberations of individual men and women. Any theory of obligation which could help deliberation about world hunger and development policies would have to overcome all these problems.

Nevertheless, nobody travelled further towards a universal theory of obligation than Kant. Even if he did not provide a map for the whole journey, he charted large stretches of it. His map may point us towards a theory of obligation which is generally accessible, yet is neither so vague and 'thin' that it cannot guide action or so bound to locally established categories of thought that it cannot criticize them. From the frontier it may be possible to see the outlines of further terrain that must be charted if the boundaries of reasoning about world hunger and poverty are to be pushed back by modes of deliberation that are generally accessible yet action-guiding. At our present frontier the well-known abstraction and individualism of Kantian ethics appear to be the worst obstacles to further exploration.[3]

4 Kantian Maxims, Partial Autonomy and Individualism

The serious difficulties faced by any theory of obligation that is both accessible and action-guiding for actual agents and agencies, yet aims to criticize established ways of thought, may be surmountable. A maverick version of Kantian ethical reasoning can start from the grids of categories with which agents and agencies are at home (so be both accessible and action-guiding for individuals and for some institutions and collectivities), but maintain the capacity to criticize received views. There is no need for critical action-centred reasoning about world hunger or poverty either to adopt the recipients' perspective of the human rights movement or to be confined to reasoning with individuals, and no reason to think that it cannot guide action. This can be shown in two steps. The first shows that an abstract starting point does not entail individualism; the second shows that it does not entail empty formalism.

Kant's ethical theory parades its abstract character in its claim to find a supreme principle of action – the Categorical Imperative – for 'rational beings as such'. Yet it was no part of his enterprise to set out the *obligations* of rational beings as such. *Wholly* rational beings would not in any case flout standards of rationality. For them no requirement of reason would impose an *obligation*; but those of limited rationality can be drawn to irrationality. Kant's theory of obligation is by definition a theory of principles of action for beings of *limited* rationality. Human beings are evidently finitely rational; but so are human institutions and collectivities. Since Kantian obligations are supposed to guide the action of agents with partial rather than idealized capacities to understand and to act, they may equally serve the deliberating of institutions and collectivities with limited rationality and powers of actions.[4] If the Categorical Imperative is relevant for partially rational and autonomous beings, it can be made relevant for institutional and collective as well as for individual deliberation. Kant's conception of the autonomy of obligation-holders assumes only partial rationality and limited powers of actions and so does not entail individualism.

Kant's theory of action also does not entail individualism. He sees action as done on *maxims* or principles of action, and proposes a 'supreme principle of morality' that requires action only on maxims that could also be adopted by others.[5] 'Action on a maxim' is usually understood as acting on a certain intention; and on many quasi-Cartesian views of intentions this would mean that individual agents could, but institutional and collective agents could not, act on maxims. Maxims can equally and perhaps more plausibly be interpreted as the *fundamental* principles which guide actions, policies and practices, whether individual, institutional or collective (Höffe, 1977; O'Neill, 1984a, 1985b). Of the many principles an action (or policy or practice) may exemplify, the maxim is basic and others are ancillary. For example, a family might habitually provide food for hungry neighbours. If their maxim is to feed their neighbours, and any other principles exemplified in so doing (such as ensuring a reputation for generosity or, less admirably, displaying wealth) are ancillary, then they would go on providing the food even if the gift was secret. However, if their fundamental principle was to gain a good reputation, the food would not be given if nobody would come to know of it.

This example shows that collectivities as well as individuals can act on maxims; and institutions can do so too. For example, a landlord who evicts a family for non-payment of rent may act on the same commercial maxim that a property company might act on in like circumstance. It is not the landlord's state of mind that is evaluated in Kantian ethical deliberation, but what he does. (He may or may not have sleepless nights or feel compunction about the eviction.) The property company will not suffer sleepless nights: but the principles that guide its action may be the very ones that an individual landlord follows. What counts in this theory of action is not the state of consciousness of the agent, but the principle that determines action or policy. The same maxim of action can guide individuals, collectivities or institutions.

It is often obscure which of the many principles that apply to some action or policy is its maxim. Introspection is not a reliable witness to the maxims on which individuals act (Kant says this repeatedly); and it is quite irrelevant to establishing the maxims of institutional or collective agents. The maxim of an act can be discovered only by finding the various circumstances on which the doing of the act is contingent. Cutting back on some aid project might, for example, be based either on a maxim of reducing donor expenditures or on one of increasing 'donor' political leverage or on one of concentrating aid where it is most needed. It may often be tempting to present policies based on the first two maxims as being guided by the third. The test of this claim is whether in fact aid for the neediest is increased or at least maintained even where over-all aid expenditure is cut or political leverage increased. Claims of good will or benevolence from government spokesmen can no more convert a policy based on either of the first two maxims into one based on the third, than could analogous individual claims about benevolent intentions. Maxims are principles of action, and neither introspection nor official briefings are always reliable in settling what the maxim of a given act or policy is. Where false or partial claims are put forward, an initial step in deliberation may be to seek a more accurate view of the maxims of current or proposed policies. This does not demand that we find some Archimedean standpoint from which total insight into the maxims of all action is possible, but only that established and establishment claims about what they are be open to query and reassessment.

5   Kantian Maxims and Principles of Obligation

A Kantian ethic need not then be committed to individualism, but it is committed to *some* abstract consideration of action. In this, however, it may not differ from more local and contextual forms of action-centred reasoning. The problem is not to get away from abstraction of all sorts, but to avoid forms of abstraction which leave ethical deliberation isolated among peaks of lofty rhetoric, without prospect of rejoining human affairs. Kant has the reputation of making this difficult. Even if we forget about wholly rational beings, many have doubted that a theory of the obligations of 'finite rational beings as such' can tell us at all concretely about the obligations of the rich to the hungry and destitute.

Kant, however, did not think that the Categorical Imperative *alone* could guide action. It is puzzling that many of his commentators over the decades have insisted that he must have meant this. The Categorical Imperative is offered only as 'the supreme principle of practical reason'. It is where practical deliberation begins – not where it ends. No agent or agency can use the Categorical Imperative except by applying it to some maxim of action. All complete Kantian deliberation requires the minor premise of practical reasoning – the proposed maxim of action – to be formulated, and then critically assessed in terms of the Categorical Imperative. Agents and agencies select the minor premises of their deliberations partly by using the grid of categories that constitutes their local idiom and moral starting point, and partly by criticizing that specification of problems, allocations of problems and claims about available action in the light of wider considerations, including ethical principles. If they did not, the maxim of their own action would be inaccessible and alien to them (as perhaps happens with agents whose self-consciousness is distorted), and the principle to which they applied the Categorical Imperative would not be the one that was fundamental to their action or policy.

Practical reasoning which uses the Categorical Imperative asks of a given, accessible maxim whether it is one that *could* be acted on by others, or whether on the contrary, it could only be adopted on the assumption that others' action is not guided by it. The central conception of Kantian ethics is that a maxim should not be acted on if it *could not* (not *should not* or *would not*) be acted on by others. Here obligations are a matter of refraining from action whose fundamental principles others cannot share. (Perhaps this is too thin and weak a foundation for ethical reasoning. That is something we cannot know until we see how much work it can do.)

This conception is related to, but not the same as, the proposed grounding of natural or moral rights in the idea of individual spheres of action in which others may not interfere. Individuals who had rights in that sense would be encapsulated in a sphere of 'self-regarding action', whose boundaries others could not justly cross. Hence acts which all have a right to do or have done must be acts which can be done by or for all. Acts falling under any description, whether fundamental or trivial, would either be assigned to that sphere or excluded from it. This would define a consistent set of rights for all circumstances. The Kantian starting point insists only that *fundamental* principles of action be internally consistent, and does not forbid action confirming to *ancillary* principles that cannot consistently be adopted by all agents and agencies. Since specific aspects of action can be ancillary to different maxims on different occasions, they will not often be either universally forbidden or universally obligatory. Universalizability is a requirement on maxims, and not on specific implementations of maxims. There are powerful reasons to expect the specific aspects of particular implications of the fundamental principles of obligation to vary with circumstances.

6   Kantian Obligations and Human Finitude

Human beings are not only of limited rationality, but physically limited. They are bodily creatures with material and other needs.[6] They occupy and consume limited and scattered portions of their world. The more specific principles on which such beings act cannot be universally or even widely acted on. Nobody can eat the very grain another eats; not everybody can live under the same roof. However, this evident and basic feature of finite embodied life does not show that the very idea of restricting action to *fundamental* principles that could be universally shared is foolish. It shows only that not all of the more specific principles an act may exemplify can be available for all. Action could still be *guided by maxims* which are possible for all.

The first move away from the very abstract Categorical Imperative, which all Kantian deliberation depends upon, is to identify maxims which could not be universally shared by any rational beings, hence not by beings of limited rationality and powers. Avoiding action on these maxims is the fundamental requirement of any Kantian theory of obligation. On Kant's own account nonuniversalizable principles, whose implementation is forbidden and whose avoidance is obligatory, include principles of coercion and deceit (the principles which justice must reject) as well as principles of disrespect, nonbeneficence and nondevelopment (the principles which our wider, imperfect obligations reject). Although these fundamental principles all require *avoidance* of certain sorts of action, their implementation often demands positive action.

Kantian deliberation cannot justify a detailed set of social and institutional or ideological forms as right for all times and all places. It begins by showing which relatively abstract principles of action (which could guide institutions, policies or action) cannot in principle be acted on by all, so ought not to guide action. It can then be extended to show more specific acts, policies and institutions either forbidden or obligatory *in a given situation* by showing either that they would constitute implementations of forbidden underlying principles in that situation (and so themselves forbidden in that situation), or that they would be essential to avoid acting on forbidden underlying principles in that situation (and so obligatory in that situation). Kantian deliberation is then doubly nonalgorithmic. First, it is a decision procedure for detecting forbidden and obligatory action, and does not aim to rank all possible actions. Secondly, its deployment in contexts of action depends upon the far from mechanical processes of working out in a given context whether specific acts, policies and institutions are ruled out or required if a particular maxim is to guide action.

Kantian deliberation is not then in principle either too abstract to guide action, or accessible only within the confines of the 'normal' political and ethical discussion of a particular social and ideological sphere. Its structure need not rule out modes of deliberation which bridge some ideological and social gaps. It remains to be seen how well it can guide deliberation about problems whose nature and remedy cuts across well-established boundaries between different spheres of life.

Although its structure is appropriate for deliberation which bridges spheres of life, Kantian deliberating might have nothing to say about problems of world hunger. Even if it can in principle overcome abstraction, it may in practice be vague. The transition from relatively indeterminate principles of obligation to more specific requirements for action in particular contexts might need information that is unavailable. Or it might be that the root idea of Kantian ethics – that of acting only on fundamental principles on which all can act – is just too weak to ground interesting conclusions. A full answer to these worries can emerge only in the context of attempting much Kantian deliberation in actual contexts of action, but a sketch of some transitions from more abstract to more contextualized debate about world hunger can suggest what may be possible.

Kantian practical deliberation begins by identifying a few relatively abstract principles which could not coherently guide the action of all members of a group of (wholly or partially) rational agents and agencies. An abstract account of Kantian principles of obligation is that they are those very general principles of action whose converse is shown nonuniversalizable. For example, if a principle of deception cannot be universally used to guide action, then the converse principle of nondeception would be among the principles of obligation. Or if a principle of coercion was similarly nonuniversalizable, then the converse principle of noncoercion would be among the principles of obligation. However, if Kantian deliberation gave up at this point, it would offer only recommendations too abstract and indeterminate to guide action. To reach action-guiding conclusions it is important to show which more specific actions are needed to avoid deceit and coercion in a particular context of action.

Kant speaks of the demand for 'outward conformity' to underlying maxims of obligation. His examples suggest, and his commentators insist, that he assumes that there is a unique set of more specific rules of action that would conform outwardly to the requirements of nondeception and noncoercion. If he does so – the textual issues are tangled – Kantian reasoning would be inaccessible and useless for deliberation that must address heterogeneous agents and agencies. Also, if Kant's view of what outward conformity to maxims of noncoercion and nondeception amounts to is a unique set of rules, as some passages suggest, and those rules could guide the action only of idealized, individual agents, then Kant's own specific ethical conclusions would be irrelevant in *all* human affairs.

Even if these traditional misgivings are an accurate assessment of parts of Kant's writings, it does not follow that a revised

Kantian pattern of ethical deliberation must be useless in the deliberations either of actual, nonidealized individuals or in those of institutions and collectivities. It could be relevant provided that there are context-sensitive ways of specifying what it takes to conform to principles such as those of noncoercion and non-deception in the actual situations in which we find ourselves.

7   Rational and Needy Beings

The Categorical Imperative forbids action which *in that context*, would constitute action on principles that cannot guide others' action, and requires action which could be guided by the contrary principles. The first stage of Kantian deliberation identifies relatively abstract principles of this sort.

These relatively abstract principles of obligation can be divided into two groups, which Kant classified under the usual headings of principles for determining *perfect duties* and those for determining *imperfect duties*. As in other ethical theories, perfect duties are seen as including justice, and imperfect duties as including beneficence. Kant is distinctive in viewing respect for others and the development of skills and talents and other capacities as equally basic imperfect duties (he is mainly concerned with *self*-development: but the point can be taken more broadly). This suggests some interesting advantages for a Kantian approach to problems of poverty and development.

The Kantian distinction between perfect and imperfect duties differs from those made in consequentialist and rights-based ethical reasoning. On the Kantian account *perfect* duty is action which is required in a given context in order to avoid acting on a nonuniversalizable fundamental principle; most such duties are duties of justice. Rules of justice can, he claimed, be worked out for any possible group of rational beings, although their content will vary: 'the problem of justice can be solved, even for a "nation of devils"' (Kant, 1795, p. 112). Even among human beings, the demands of justice will vary with circumstances. There is no reason to think that justice under human conditions has the same content as justice among devils, and no reason to think that the specific rules of justice are timelessly the same under all human circumstances. Justice in conditions of scarcity may be quite unlike justice in conditions of abundance.

Kant mainly discusses two fundamental principles of justice.

These are the principles of noncoercion and nondeception, to which the action of *any* rational beings must conform if governed by universalizable principles. Coercion, whatever its specific form, pre-empts others' action; it treats others as things or tools and exacts their compliance. Any 'consent' or 'agreement' given to coercive action, which pre-empts the victims' capacities to choose and act, is spurious. The victims are not genuinely treated as agents, who would be able to consent to or to refuse the other's action. A maxim of coercion could not underlie all action, since those whose agency is undercut cannot themselves coerce. Action which is fundamentally based on coercion must be selective and so forbidden on Kantian grounds. It allows the coercer a position of privilege denied the victim.

Maxims of deception too cannot be universally adopted: deceptions work only in contexts where most communication is nondeceptive. Deception undercuts others' cognition, it treats others as things or tools, and extracts their agreement. Any 'consent' or 'agreement' given to deceptive action, which pre-empts the 'victims' cognitive capacities, is bogus. The victims are not genuinely treated as agents. A maxim of deception could not underlie all action, since deception works only where conditions of trust are established and maintained. Action which is fundamentally based on deception must be selective and so forbidden on Kantian grounds. It allows the deceiver a position of privilege denied the victim.

These argument sketches focus *only* on maxims. Notoriously, many seemingly innocuous more specific aspects of action also cannot be universalized. Since human activity is the activity of embodied and dependent beings, whose use of the material world pre-empts one another's use of it, we cannot even imagine what it would be for all specific aspects of human action to be universalizable.[7] The Categorical Imperative can only provide – as Kant supposed it could – a principle for rejecting certain maxims; it cannot by itself discriminate among ancillary, specific principles of action. Sometimes a *fundamental* commitment to noncoercion might *require* action which in subsidiary respects was coercive or deceptive. Even if Kant was personally drawn to rigourism, as some passages suggest, an interpretation of the Kantian enterprise which commits it to rigourism – the view that all permissible principles of action (not just fundamental ones) must be universalizable – is a nonstarter, both for Kantian and for wider reasons.

It does not follow from the fact that the Categorical Imperative only discriminates fundamental principles of action that Kantian ethics cannot guide action and be accessible to agents and agencies who are at home with local and specific grids of categories. Yet another traditional and reiterated claim about Kantian ethics is that it is not after all rigouristic, but (on the contrary) too 'formalistic' to guide action. If it is only fundamental principles, such as 'do not coerce' and 'do not deceive' that can be shown morally unacceptable, is not anything permitted in practice? Any act or policy can be redescribed in various ways that do not mention deception or coercion. The Newspeak of our century has shown an appalling talent for putting an acceptable face on odious policies and actions, and if anything is permitted, nothing is required, and the whole Kantian enterprise is empty.

However, fundamental principles or maxims are not 'worthy intentions' which can be claimed by lip-service alone. They are the guiding principles of action and policy. In specific circumstances noncoercion and nondeception may be serious constraints on permissible action. To show how they constrain action needs an account of specificatory reasoning in actual deliberation. Kantian ethics is action-guiding only if agents can answer questions of the form 'is this policy non-deceptive in these circumstances?' or 'would such an institution be noncoercive in these circumstances?' They must assess whether political and economic institutions and policies are fundamentally nondeceptive and noncoercive in particular circumstances, and meet other fundamental standards of obligatory action. Specificatory reasoning can relate fundamental, relatively abstract standards and principles of action to actual human contexts. It has to take account of what is actually required to avoid coercing or deceiving beings who are not only of limited rationality, but limited in other ways.

If perfect duty requires action, policies and institutions that neither coerce nor deceive in fundamental ways, then account must be taken of human vulnerability to coercion or deception of sorts that might not affect ideally rational agents and agencies. Human agents are vulnerable to damage both to material intervention and to material needs; they can therefore be coerced in many ways which would not affect ideally rational or disembodied beings. Since human agents are embodied, and so located in their world, they have only limited, perspective knowledge –

they comprehend their world through limited grids of categories. They are therefore vulnerable to many forms of deception that would not affect ideally rational or disembodied beings. Hence the specific policies and institutions which might be just in actual human situations must do more than rule out a limited range of coercive and deceptive forms of action that undermine any sort of rational agency. The details of human justice must take account of the most basic needs that must be met if other human beings are not to be fundamentally deceived or coerced. Any just global order must *at least* meet standards of material justice and provide for the basic material needs in whose absence all human beings are overwhelmingly vulnerable to coercion and deception.

Human vulnerability also entails that justice cannot be the only human obligation. There are also principles of imperfect duty to others for finitely rational beings who are limited in various other ways. For disembodied, mutually invulnerable rational beings who did not depend on one another either physically or psychologically, there might be no principles of imperfect duty. Provided that they acted justly, they could not infringe on one another's autonomy. They could make their choices and do their own thing (whatever that might be), provided that others' action conformed to principles of perfect duty. The problem of justice not only can be solved for a 'nation' of such invulnerable rational beings: it is the only problem that need be solved to discover what obligations they could have.

However, human action is vulnerable even when just institutions and policies have been established. It remains vulnerable both because the practice of just institutions may fall short of their principles and because even those who live in circumstances of justice are often unable to act without others' help. A Kantian account of imperfect duty requires conformity to principles of mutual respect and help and development, without which the agency of needy and limited beings is insecure. Principles of disrespect, of neglect of beneficence and neglect of talents too are non-universalizable, although in a slightly different sense than the principles of noncoercion and nondeception. Rational and needy beings *could* all of them act on principles of disrespect, neglect of beneficence and neglect of talents. However, since each acts with limited capacities, and knows that any sustained and autonomous action by needy and rational beings standardly requires some respect and cooperation from others, and the development of some talents, each must ensure that some help is given and some talents are developed. Hence any agent whose fundamental maxim it is to disrespect, to refuse help or to neglect talents acts on a nonuniversalizable maxim, so violates obligations.

It does not follow from this commitment that certain more specific principles of beneficence and fostering of talents are obligatory in all possible contexts. Since the form taken by basic needs differs considerably, and capacities to meet them and to develop talents vary even more, the specific demands of obligations of respect, beneficence and the development of talents cannot be stated abstractly but must be worked out for specific contexts of action. Even the rules of justice are not timeless; and the demands of respect, beneficence and development of talents may be yet more varied. Nevertheless, the next chapter can outline some implications of Kantian conceptions of obligation for problems of world hunger and poverty.

Justice can come to seem the sole ethical requirement of the public domain if we take an idealized and inaccurate view of human rationality and other human capacities. Beneficence can come to seem the whole of ethics if the human condition is seen not as one where partial autonomy may be inadequate when needs are unmet, but as one in which conflicting desires must be aggregated. If human life is basically needy it is not surprising that ethical theories which conflate need with desire (like utilitarianism) or overlook it entirely (like many rights-based conceptions of justice) have difficulty in determining obligations towards those whose lives are warped by need. A theory which makes human autonomy (in its actual, partial forms) and human needs (in their actual, pressing variety) central, and that provides an account *both* of justice *and* of beneficence, may be more accessible and better able to guide action and policy that affects the risk and course of world hunger.

Notes

1   Sometimes obligations are picked out in reifying ways: we speak of obligations of fidelity or loyalty or friendship. However, while reifying accounts of rights easily suggest that the right would be fulfilled by getting and possessing some unitary good, reifying accounts of obligations do not so readily suggest images of possession and transfer.

2 Kant discusses judgement in numerous passages. The distinction between determinant and reflective is also repeatedly drawn (Kant, 1781, 1790). Recent discussions of reflective judging can be found in Arendt (1982), especially commentary by Beiner, Guyer (1979) and O'Neill (1984b, 1985a).

3 There is plenty of textual warrant for this traditional view, in spite of Kant's copious discussions of judgement and casuistry. The text of the *Groundwork* (Kant, 1785), which intersperses discussion of the obligations of 'finite rational beings' with examples appropriate to individual action in late eighteenth-century Königsberg, without making explicit transitions, provides ample ground for it. Questions of interpretation are bracketed in this discussion, and some of the positions labelled 'Kantian' are extensions or developments of positions to be found in the Kantian texts. Some of the textual questions are broached in O'Neill (1984a, 1985a, 1985b, 1985c). The *Groundwork* is no *introductory* work on ethics, but a complex and ambitious discussion which sketches a wholly abstract theory of rational action, a more determinate theory of the obligations of finite rational beings and a skimpy account of human obligations in specific circumstances and relationships.

4 Since the capacities to understand and powers of action of individual agents often differ from those of institutional and collective agencies, we may expect some of their obligations to differ, just as we expect the obligations of individuals whose capacities for action are limited only in the standard ways to differ from the obligations of those with more reduced capacities such as children, the retarded and invalids.

5 This is a reasonable approximation of the idea that lies behind the various distinct formulations of the Categorical Imperative. The Formula of Universal Law states explicitly that action should be on a maxim 'through which you can at the same time will that it should become a universal law'; the Formula of the End in Itself demands action which does not 'use others as means, but always at the same time as an end'. If 'others' are understood as other finite rational beings, then the first formula forbids action which is not in principle left open for other finitely rational beings to do or refrain from doing; the second formula forbids action which usurps others' agency, so also does not in principle leave that action open for others to do or refrain from doing (O'Neill, 1984b, 1985c).

6 It is beyond the scope of this revision of Kantian ethics to provide a complete theory of human needs. Fortunately, only the least controversial assumptions are required. The needs that constrain the obligations of partially rational and needy beings include *at least* those whose neglect undercuts all possibility of sustained autonomous action. Only the most fundamental material and social needs have to be met if a life including some autonomous action is to be possible. So, for example, basic subsistence and security (food, water, safety, some minimal physical and social skills) are needed for any sustained life involving autonomous action. There may be other needs without which action would be restricted but not impossible; these are not discussed here. Cf. the discussion of 'basic needs' in Shue (1981), and the broader discussion of needs in Weil (1949).

7 Only a physicalist principle for act individuation could make a mutually exclusive partitioning of the world, such as theories of rights require, possible. It is hard to show the point of the highly intricate spaces which would have to be assigned to individuals to provide them even with standard rights such as rights to access to public places and rights of free speech within the terms of a physicalist grounding of rights. Metaphysical materialism and common old greedy materialism are closer than appears on the surface.

8
Obligations to the Poor

> All human beings are bound by identicial obligations,
> although these are performed in different ways according to
> circumstances. . . . The obligation is only performed if . . .
> expressed in a real, not a fictitious, way; and this can only be
> done through the medium of Man's earthly needs . . . it is an
> eternal obligation to the human being not to let him suffer
> from hunger when one has the chance of coming to his
> assistance. (Weil, 1949, pp. 4–6)

1 Obligations of Justice, Beneficence and Development

The Kantian ethic just outlined is fitted in various ways to guide
ethical deliberation about problems of famine and world hunger.
To begin with, it takes an abstract, but nonidealized, conception
of human agency and so can be widely accessible to human agents
and agencies of divergent outlook and formation. Here agency
goes with power to bring about changes. Secondly, the obligation
not to act unjustly – to act in accord with maxims of noncoercion
and nondeception – is universal, rather than attached to specific
roles or agencies. Thirdly, obligations to respect, help and develop
talents and other capacities are also universal. Fourthly, Kantian
obligations can be connected in actual deliberation to the varied
grids of more specific categories used by different agents and
agencies in differing circumstances. Hence its more specific implications can be made accessible in particular contexts to those
whose action is needed. However, the price of this contextual
accessibility need not be cooption by established and establishment conceptions of the problems of world hunger and the
solutions of development policy. Kantian deliberation operates
with a critical theory of the specification and allocation of prob-

lems and available action. Rival accounts of problems, of their allocation and of possible lines of action and their limits, and of the implications which fundamental principles of obligation are thought to have in a determinate context, can be understood, challenged and made more widely accessible.

Since actual deliberation is a matter for those who can act, the specific implementation of obligations by institutional policy and collective and individual action will vary with context. Although the conclusions of this essay will not be a set of detailed policy recommendations and proposals for action, some implications of a Kantian approach to world hunger and development can be outlined.

The most general implication is that Kantian justice could be sought and achieved only by far-reaching political activity which transforms the basic principles of economic and social structures. The present international economic order is patently an institutional structure whose normal operation does not eliminate coercion or deception, but often institutionalizes them. It also standardly fails to respect, or to provide the help or development of talents needed for lives that can include autonomous action. Hence a transformation of the structure of agency is required by justice. This is recognized in many recent works in development studies (Brandt, 1980, 1983; IGBA, 1983; Alston and Tomasevski, 1984). In many actual contexts 'normal' political activity cannot achieve such changes. Hence the work of justice may often have more to do with transformation of established grids of categories and received outlook than with 'normal' politics. However, such ideological and political transformations would only meet Kantian standards if they were themselves reasoned shifts from a 'moral starting point' to a revised ethical position. Transformation based on *mere* conversion or indoctrination has no part in Kantian ethical deliberation; and forced conversions or brain-washing coerce and so are unjust.

On a Kantian account, respect, the provision of needed help and the development of needed talents and other capacities are not subordinate ethical concerns whose omission is not wrong. Imperfect obligations are obligations. Agents and agencies whose action fundamentally fails in respect, neglects needed help or the development of needed talents and capacities do wrong, although no others have rights to specific action. These obligations are once again universal, although the forms that each will take must vary with context. Kantian respect allows agents to act for themselves. Kantian beneficence supplies help needed if they are to be able to act (it lays no stress on providing enjoyment rather than needed help). Kantian development of talents supplies skills and capacities, including institutionally embodied capacities, that are needed for autonomous action. The specific requirements of such obligations will always vary with context. Clearly, they will differ in circumstances of poverty and institutionalized injustice and in circumstance of justice or abundance.

Rational but needy beings *know* that they cannot act without others' respect and at times will need others' help and to rely on developed talents and capacities. So if their action is based on neglecting any of these, they act on nonuniversalizable maxims. Agents and agencies who are not self-sufficient (and those with limited rationality and powers are never self-sufficient) *cannot* will (let alone want) to find themselves part of a world in which respect, help and the development of skills and capacities are universally neglected. Since no agent or agency can meet all needs or develop all talents (so much follows from human finitude), obligations to help those in need and to develop needed skills and capacities are unavoidably selective.

Neither respect nor providing needed help nor fostering needed skills and capacities can substitute for justice. Justice is embodied in public institutions and policies which secure freedom from deep forms of coercion and deception. Circumstances of justice are lacking so long as material and social needs are so great that coercion and deception are not merely easy but virtually unavoidable. In an unjust and needy world, there is more scope and need for respect and help to those in need and more potential for developing required skills. None of these activities, however, can provide the institutional conditions which systematically meet material needs and guarantee the absence of coercion and deception.

2   Hunger and Material Justice

The central demand of Kantian justice is negative: that action, policies and institutions not be based on or conform to fundamental principles of coercion or deception. These standards can be applied in evaluating principles which underlie the present international economic and political order, and those on which specific agencies, policies and institutions are based. They can also be used in deliberation about proposed institutions, policies and acts. Such deliberations must try to show what it would take to embody principles of noncoercion and nondeception in the actual charters and operation of institutions, and in social and economic practices and policies, as well as in the activity of individual and collective agents. It may begin by considering agents' and agencies' claims about principles which underlie their practice and action, but the process of deliberation may later lead beyond agents' grids of categories and their initial formulation of maxims and plans of action.

Action-centred reasoning, as we saw in Chapter 7, section 4, does not have to be agent-centred reasoning. A company might initially represent its dealing with representatives of a poverty-stricken country as guided by standard and acceptable negotiating practice, appropriately described in terms of standard commercial categories. The management might insist that there was nothing either coercive or deceptive, and so nothing unjust, in the negotiating. However, others might think that the desperation of those with whom the deal was made meant that it amounted to a coercive 'offer they could not refuse', and so that its 'acceptance' was no proof of noncoercion. If the maxim which *actually* governed the bargaining was coercive, the deal struck would exploit others unjustly. Seen in a wider context, adherence to standard forms of commercial bargaining, which might not coerce either the ideally rational or the materially self-sufficient, may be fundamentally coercive. Negotiators coerce unless they leave opening for others, however desperate their actual circumstances, to refuse as well as to accept their offer.

Similar points can be made about reliance on standard forms of wage-bargaining and contracting in circumstances where those with whom contracts are made are too vulnerable or poor to refuse the terms offered, however low the wages or dangerous the work, or however harsh the terms of a contract. Employment and trading is exploitation if it is accepted only because it is 'an offer that cannot be refused'. It is still exploitation when the outward form is scrupulously contractual: it is *fundamental* principles of action that are of concern in Kantian ethics (O'Neill, 1984a, 1985b, 1985c).

Many basic features of contemporary economic and political forms, both national and international, are ostensibly designed to prevent coercion and deception. A standard rationale for capitalist economic forms, for democratic political institutions and for regulating global problems through negotiations between sovereign states and international agencies is that these institutional forms neither coerce nor deceive; but these arrangements would be just in Kantian terms only if they were *fundamentally* noncoercive and nondeceptive. It is not enough that they build in some, possibly superficial, barriers to coercion, such as contractual forms or elements of individual decision-making. If the context and the content of individual decisions is determined by social and economic structures which even sometimes rely on others' need in order to secure 'consent' or 'agreement', these arrangements may be fundamentally coercive and deceptive.

There are many reasons for fearing that some fundamental principles of contemporary political and economic arrangements are coercive and deceptive. Yet this is often submerged rather than salient in discussions of democratic political forms and market economies. However, choosing in the context of market economies and democratic polities does not guarantee that actual capacities to understand and powers of action have been respected. Respect for rational capacities is only superficial when the agenda of problems and range of responses is determined by aspects of the political and social structure which lie beyond challenge and investigation, or when the range of economic decisions is fixed by processes that are closed to challenge or change. Respect for others' powers to act or refuse is only superficial if outward forms of negotiation and contract merely impose arrangements which would be rejected except by those whose need is desperate. Unfortunately, the outward forms of negotiation, contract and consent may not secure freedom from coercion or deceit when one party to a transaction is rich, powerful and informed and the other poor, powerless and uninformed. Ordinary legal and commercial standards are often well observed by government agencies and grain merchants during acute famines: and yet locally 'available' grain that could save lives may be hoarded and sold when the market is highest, so raising the death toll (Sen, 1981; Shepherd, 1975). A Kantian conception of justice would require not that 'normal' political and ethical discourse employ a grid of categories which stresses individual choosing and freedom of inquiry and expression, but that a revised 'moral starting point' (which might be reached by probing this grid) make noncoercion and nondeception fundamental.

What would it take to bring the present international economic and political order closer to these standards of justice? Answers to this question must take account of the varied ways in which human agents whose needs are unmet are vulnerable to forms of deception and coercion, including some which would not affect ideally rational or self-sufficient agents. Human beings begin by being physically vulnerable. They are damaged by hunger, disease and cold, and coerced by their prospect. (They are in addition vulnerable in deep ways to one another's disdain and disregard: not all human needs are material needs.[1]) If material needs are not reliably met, the forms of uncoerced and undeceived choosing are a skimpy and formalistic substitute for fundamentally noncoercive and nondeceptive forms of life. A just global economic and political order would then have to be one designed to meet material needs. (It might fail to do so if global scarcity could not be averted.) It would be embodied in economic and political structures which do not institutionalize coercion or deception and so respect rationality and autonomy *in the vulnerable forms in which they are actually found*, rather than in the idealized forms of political and economic theory.

A just global order would have to consist of institutions and policies whose underlying principles do not neglect human, including material, needs under actual conditions. Rather than developing the economic implications of individual rights, or of aggregate benefit, a Kantian conception of material justice would begin with ways of organizing both production and distribution to meet needs, including material needs, which destroy capacities or power to act autonomously. (Other aspects of material justice might have to do with principles for distributing any surplus, or for avoiding concentrations of economic power that are likely to reintroduce the threat of need.) Many different arrangements may be adequate to secure material justice. However, any set of institutions, policies and practices which provides a just relationship to the material world would have to include certain features.

Among these features are the following. First, since the material goods by which human needs are met are mostly *produced* goods, just economic structures must provide for their production. Secondly, since human needs are recurrent, just economic structures must provide for sustained production, hence for their own reproduction, and avoid damage or degradation of the environment that would damage the possibility of a just economic order in the future. Thirdly, a just set of institutions must secure a distribution which meets autonomy-destroying needs. Since human beings are rarely self-sufficient in material respects, and vary in productive capacity and opportunity, a just distribution is not likely to arise spontaneously from an adequate organization of production. Different contemporary conceptions of economic justice propose different ways of combining the productive and distributive aspects of material justice. Capitalist economic conceptions stress the difficulty of securing production if workers and investors are not given strong individual incentives; socialist economic conceptions stress the difficulty of securing distributions which meet needs if production and distribution are not socially – usually centrally – controlled. Many actual economic systems compromise. It is neither simple nor obvious what has to be done to construct institutions and policies which meet both the productive and the distributive requirements for material justice; but it is at least clear that ideal-typical capitalist institutions may fail, because they provide no guarantee that distribution will meet needs, and that ideal-typical socialist institutions may fail, because they provide no guarantee that production will meet needs. It is idle to seek to supply each according to his need unless there are enough material goods of the right sorts to do so. Maximal production may not be needed to secure material justice, which (as argued here) demands only that material *needs* be met (so that agents can be secure from fundamental coercion and deception), and not that high standards of living or of satisfaction of desires be achieved. Various modified capitalist and socialist arrangements, as they have actually developed, have shown the potential to secure the Kantian conception of material justice *within the confines of some nation states*. (There is more doubt about their ability to secure other aspects of justice even within those confines.)

However, no contemporary international political and economic arrangements have yet shown that they can secure global material justice. The urgency of world hunger and poverty, and the vast number of people whose material and other needs are unmet, and who consequently have neither the capacities nor the power to act autonomously, suggests that this aim may exceed the capacities of present 'normal', established economic and political processes. If so the terms of 'normal' political and ethical debate may also be inadequate to these problems. This does not, however, mean that currently accessible grids of categories should be instantly rejected and replaced. Wholly revised economic and social concepts and theories might be inaccessible to many agents and agencies whose action is needed. Terms of debate that could guide the action only of ideally rational agents – like some forms of utilitarian and rights-based reasoning which reject established categories and social theories – cannot help the deliberations of actual agents and agencies.

A *process* of debate, criticism, reassessment and revision of currently established grids of concepts has to be located within and between agents and agencies who have the capacities and power to remedy (or exacerbate) others' need. A Kantian conception of material justice can provide direction to such debate. It can offer reasons for rejecting any account of the problems of world hunger, their allocation and their remedy, which merely mirrors existing economic or power relations, or which would be appropriate only for idealized agents with limitless capacities and no unmet needs. It could also avoid the assimilation of justice into a utilitarian programme of global beneficence which may give intense desires priority over urgent needs.

This approach to material justice provides a critical view of some current economic categories and claims. For example, when certain transfers are termed 'aid' it is implied that they are not required by justice. When others are termed 'loans' it is suggested that the transferred resources were previously justly allocated, and that those who receive the loan may justly be required to pay interest. When transfers to the hungry are described as 'gifts' they are not seen as required by justice. We know that these matters *could* be differently understood, because they are differently understood within certain national states. Even in capitalist societies, where commercial categories provide one standard way of looking at the world, transfer payments made by processes of taxation are seldom seen either as 'aid' or as 'gifts'. Nor on the other hand are they seen (except by a few libertarians) as unjust confiscation. They are part and parcel of a just social order which meets needs, and so forestalls the coercion and deceit of those whose needs are unmet.

An analogous revision of accepted categories on an international scale is evidently hard. It certainly cannot be achieved by overlooking the reality of the present political divisions between sovereign national states. To do that would guarantee debate that is inaudible where it needs to be heard. Internationalist sentiment is too often heady with rhetoric, but absent in the operating categories of agents and agencies that set the agenda and make the decisions. Theoretical rearticulation sometimes precedes institutional transformation. At times the order may be reversed: textbook and 'realist' views of capitalist economies or national interests may use more rigid and abstract economic and political concepts than those with responsibility for action find useful. 'The socially responsible corporation' may be more alien to neo-classical economic theory than to some modern businesses. Rigid nationalist sentiment may have become more suspect to some actual agents and agencies than appears from the national categories that bound 'normal' political discourse, and the torrent of nationalist rhetoric that washes through political discussions (Hoffmann, 1981, p. 39).

Advocacy of changes in established categories and received views merges into increasingly political commitment that is 'closer to the action'. Rather than action being available and required only of those whose roles in current institutions confer obligations, Kantian justice consists of *universal* obligations to refrain from action based on maxims of coercion or deception, whose content varies with the capacities and powers that agents and agencies have in particular contexts. Hence there are literally innumerable contexts of action. Agents and agencies who contribute to economic or social life in any way from manufacturing to education, from journalism to government service, or from professional service to activity in the women's or trade union movement, have opportunities to advocate and further conceptual, institutional and legal forms that reduce the power and acceptance of unjust arrangements. The specific arguments and campaigns open to particular agents or agencies will vary with their social location and responsibilities. So too will the particular measures needed for progress towards global material justice.

For some it may be possible to act in very direct ways to help meet the needs of the poorest. They may be able to work for trade measures that secure export markets for poor countries, or provide guaranteed prices for commodities on which some impoverished regions depend. They may work through – or against – national or multinational institutions to help secure larger and more effective 'aid' payments and projects. They may be able to prevent the export of capital intensive technologies that destroy work opportunities for the poor (such as the import of combine harvesters to Bangladesh), and to advocate or secure more investment in appropriate technology and rural development whose benefits will be more widely shared. They may be able to prevent the export of hazardous products or processes (such as pesticides, or asbestos processing without health safeguards, which are banned in the developed world), or to insist on appropriate safety standards and compensation for damage already done. They may try to prevent transnational corporations from shifting operations, or 'repatriating' capital, in ways that damage fragile economies, or to guarantee that they contribute to the tax revenues of the countries where they operate, and see that they do not inflict ecological or other damage. They may be able to work to secure grain reserves and more stable cereal prices. No theory of justice can determine fully which actions are open for a given agent or agency at a given time. It can provide only a starting point – a major premise – for deliberation and action that leads towards a less unjust international economic and political order.

Much activity that contributes to material justice is more indirect. It is not necessarily less effective. Very few of those who contribute to change of *any* sort can later pick out certain changes as 'their' achievement. Even the most prized 'individual' successes of sporting, artistic and intellectual life often depend on team work, opportunity, public opinion and collective effort. The widespread perception that 'nothing can be done' is probably more accurately described as a belief that no *individual* can be *sure* of making a significant difference to the fundamental principles on which global social and economic structures are based. This is true; but it would be grounds for despair or apathy only if it was also reasonable to believe that no action (individual, institutional or collective) could (whether we know it or not) make a significant difference. Past progress in much of the world towards social and economic structures increasingly able to meet human needs suggests that this belief is groundless. Indirect action by means of education, publicity, normal 'political' involvement and maintaining a clear and public commitment to standards of justice may produce enormous changes. Often, however, it is obscure who or what has produced fundamental change in public affairs; and even when it is not, changes can seldom be laid at any individual's door. One harmful corollary of an excessively individual conception of human agency is that too many look only for demonstrable individual success, experience a sense of failure when this eludes them, and may take less part in pursuing goals that can only be achieved collectively and through institutional action.

A Kantian theory of justice of this contextual sort suggests in broad outline what fundamental principles of material justice – those of noncoercion and nondeception – might amount to among agents and agencies whose capacities are not those of ideal rationality, but rather the partial capacities for autonomous action of actual human life. Material justice is not the whole of justice, and there are many other obligations which would have to be met in circumstances of complete justice. Nothing has been said here about the nonmaterial needs of partially rational agents, and what it would take to find social and economic forms that met them. In particular nothing has been said about institutional forms which would avoid fundamental forms of deception in areas where coercion is not the main issue. A fuller account of Kantian justice would have to outline the requirements not only for material but for political and social justice.

Political and social justice are not, of course, irrelevant to world hunger and development. If material justice needs material security, and so requires economic production and distribution which meets certain standards, many sorts of social and political organization may be unjust even when they do not affect material needs directly, because they do so indirectly. We know quite well, for example, that the social relationships of feudal villages and of nineteenth-century factory towns and of twentieth-century labour camps are likely to be incompatible with material justice. So too are political forms which thwart needed production and distribution. The justice and injustice of social and political forms is often a matter of fundamentally coercive and deceptive structures which prevent or limit action *even when material needs are met*. A wider consideration of social and political justice, and of the more 'transparent' institutions and ideologies needed if fundamental deception is to be avoided, is vital in discussion of world hunger because it might complete a picture of material justice, as well as in its own right. It deserves more discussion here, but must mainly be crowded out. However, since population questions are vital for problems of hunger and famine, they cannot be bracketed.

3 Justice and Population Policy

A Kantian framework can also be used in deliberating about the justice of population policies. Individuals may, no doubt, act wrongly in matters of procreation as elsewhere: they may coerce or deceive one another over contraception, conception and the rearing of children. Justice here, however, depends mainly on the fundamental principles of institutions and policies which affect population growth.

Once again a Kantian approach makes salient some aspects of population problems which are less central in other ethical theories. Utilitarian discussions of population are much concerned with optimum population size. This has particular interest for a theory which makes right action depend on calculation either of average or of total utility. Since changing the numbers of persons will most probably change both, it seems that optimum future numbers cannot be known *until* at least some utilitarian calculation of right action is complete. Yet it also seems that all calculation must *presuppose* knowledge of actual future numbers. Interesting and paradoxical problems emerge when average or total benefit can be changed merely by changing future numbers (Parfit, 1984).

In a rights framework discussion has tended to centre on the limits and allocation of a supposed right to procreate. There is general agreement that population goals cannot justly use coercion (e.g. forced sterilization or abortion), but disagreement on whether procreation rights can justly be restricted in other ways. Are these rights to be exercised with the aid of abstinence, or of some (but perhaps not other) methods of contraception? May their exercise depend on (voluntary) abortion (in any or in all circumstances) or even on certain types of infanticide? Some rights theorists take a rather abstract view of individual agents, and see in infants' restricted capacities to act no reason to consider them as having lesser rights. Hence they have tended to argue that abortion is wrong. Others, however, have argued that a foetus has no right to be brought to term unless the woman whose body it inhabits consents (Sumner, 1981). The allocation of a right to procreate is also disputed: is it a woman's right to choose, as many feminists argue, or one that belongs to that curious hybrid, the 'individual couple'? Other rights-oriented debates about population concern the sorts of public support that may or must be given to procreative rights as variously construed. May public funds be used to support family planning services, but not to support abortion services, as was argued by representatives of President Reagan's administration at the 1984 International Conference on Population in Mexico City? If women have a right to abortion, have they any right to publicly supported health care which provides abortion services?

From a Kantian perspective these debates overlook the population issues that matter most for questions of world hunger. The utilitarian debates are often too abstract to connect to actual situations and predicaments. Calculation of optimal population policies in the abstract has theoretical interest but is distant from problems over procreative decisions or over population policies as these may arise for actual agents and agencies. Concern with procreative rights (however construed) assumes that justice requires that 'individual' procreative decisions be neither coerced nor deceived. Neither approach considers whether the fundamental principles of the institutional and social context in which procreative decisions are made are either coercive or deceptive.

Procreation appears so evidently to be the concern of individual agents and of small collectivities (couples, families and perhaps certain clans or larger communities) that it is easy to overlook the fact that even the most autonomous procreative decisions are made in a context established by the fundamental principles of wider social and economic institutions and policies. There is nothing new in this. The regularities studied by demographers show clearly that fertility has long reflected far more than individual decisions taken within biological limits. Varied social institutions and practices have nearly always kept human fertility below its theoretical limit. Patterns of late or early marriage or weaning, traditions of celibacy, conceptions of kinship and inheritance, as well as public policies that provide medical care or penalize the prolific, or reward and subsidize them selectively, all affect fertility. The first question to raise in population ethics is not about individual procreative decisions, but about the underlying principles which structure the contexts in which those decisions are made.

Population growth cannot be a matter of indifference for a theory of obligation which takes actual needs seriously. Needs increase with numbers, and if resources cannot or do not grow with numbers, scarcity will grow and so coercion and deception become harder to avoid. Just institutions, policies and actions must aim to meet sufficient needs to forestall the greater vulnerability to coercion and deception that unmet needs produce. If not all the needs of a rapidly growing population can be met by increased production and by more just distribution, policies which slow rates of population growth will be required for global justice. This seems likely to be the case in the late twentieth century, and far beyond. UN forecasts predict a rise from 4.4 to 6.1 billion between 1980 and 2000 (Brandt, 1980). Since births now hugely exceed deaths, and mortality cannot be increased without unjust coercion, even great success in reducing fertility will not stabilize numbers for many decades.

Such success is unlikely to be produced by responsible parental decisions alone. Parental decisions are taken in social and economic context, by agents with a specific outlook, expectations and information, and with access to certain types of contraceptive and medical services. The institutional and ideological framework of those decisions might be varied in many ways, while still leaving many procreative decisions open to parental choice. Increases in child survival and prosperity mark one change in the context of procreative decisions which is standardly associated with a *demographic transition* to smaller families; reducing the subjection of women is another. However, traditional routes to slower population growth are slow, and not likely to achieve prosperity with present rates of population increase.

Various institutional changes could alter the context of many procreative decisions. In one context raising the age of marriage might be effective; in another it might be crucial to bring home the reality of reduced child mortality, and to show traditional conceptions of desirable family size obsolete. Almost everywhere transformations of women's lives and opportunities are important. Those whose only opportunity for fulfilment within a life of poverty and burdens lies in traditional maternal achievement have little reason to have fewer children (Brandt, 1980, p. 60). Contraceptive services can help those who come to want smaller families to have them. None of these policies works by coercing procreative decisions.

However, the prospect of population growth (and the methods of population control appearing in some parts of the world) are alarming enough to raise the question of coercion. If noncoercive public policies fail to reduce population growth, would more coercive measures be unjust? Kantian justice rejects *fundamental* reliance on coercion or deception, but in harsh circumstances lesser coercion might be the only way to avoid fundamental coercion. If it was clear that the fundamental coercion of widespread destitution and hunger could not be avoided without limited coercion of procreative decisions, a case might be made for limited coercion. However, the case could only be plausible when other less coercive ways of avoiding or averting fundamental coercion and deception had been exhausted. The neo-Malthusian view that those with plenty may hang on to it while others with too little have their reproduction controlled depends upon an idealized, and unjust, conception of property rights. If just economic institutions produce and distribute goods in ways likely to meet needs, they are not likely to endorse property relationships that allow hoarding while others are in need or unable to feed their children.

In a Kantian approach to population problems, justice is mainly a matter of ensuring that public institutions and policies are not based either on coercion or on deception. Social and economic institutions which set just bounds on procreative decisions may go far to curb population growth without coercive intervention in individual decisions. If such policies fail, and just productive and redistributive measures too cannot meet needs, direct coercion of procreative decisions would not be unjust. Such emergencies would arise only when recklessly fertile people persist in having children whose needs could not be met, by their parents or by others, either by increasing or by reallocating resources. Such procreators act on a maxim that cannot be widely shared without exacerbating needs and so increasing injustice. Preventing such reckless procreation would coerce less than would failing to prevent it. Deterring procreation which is likely to produce unmeetable needs requires lesser coercions for the sake of avoiding greater ones; but no coercion could be justified to avoid a fall in the standard of life of those who are not materially needy. Emergency measures are for emergencies.

4   Hunger, Help and Development

Justice, in the version of Kantian ethics explored here, is a matter of finding the fundamental principles which must underlie the action of agents and agencies who do not preclude other agents and agencies from acting on the same fundamental principles. A Kantianly just world would be one whose economic, social and political structures were based on universalizable principles. It need not be a world of economic or social or political uniformity, since many different modes of social organization might meet the standards of justice. (Even the fundamental principles have to be *universalizable*, not *universal*.) Even if the public domain were organized on such principles, and even if individual action did not introduce injustice, such a human world would be no more than a just world. A 'nation of devils' (or rational economic men) could attain this much. A more complete account of human excellence needs also to leave room for kindness and generosity, for love and friendship, and for the development of full human potentiality. Kantian ethics has often been castigated for its insensitivity here.

Kant's own account of this side of human life is that it too is a matter of action which conforms to certain fundamental principles. However, in this case the principles are not defined by the demand that we avoid fundamental principles that cannot be universally shared. That is the Kantian account only of principles of *perfect* duty. Principles of *imperfect* duty are principles which *could* be rejected by all partially rational beings without inconsistency, but which such beings could not, whatever their specific desires, rationally aim for. Partially rational, embodied beings are all too aware of their insufficiency and vulnerability, that they have needs which they cannot be sure of meeting unaided. Even in a materially just society, which is structured to leave nobody wholly vulnerable to deception or coercion, human beings standardly have quite limited capacities to act autonomously. Since actual human beings are not self-sufficient, they (unlike idealized rational beings) could never rationally seek a merely just society. Since they also have reason to fear that many present social institutions are not based on just principles, and that even those that are just in principle often fall short in practice, they must also seek to secure traditions and habits of action that go beyond justice and provide for mutual respect, help and the development of skills and capacities.

Kantian respect and beneficence are expressed in action which aims to secure others' agency when their capacities are inadequate or threatened. In an unjust world, where needs go unmet, imperfect duty too may have to focus on meeting needs, since unmet needs are then the greatest impediment to action. In a society with just institutions which operated imperfectly, imperfect duty might also often be a matter of meeting needs, since needs would be sporadically unmet. In a just society, with few failures to meet needs, imperfect duty might seldom have to focus on unmet needs, and could turn to making good lesser impediments to action. At present, when institutional structures are far from just, imperfect duty may often be the only, if incomplete, response to human needs. Respect, and beneficence in present conditions may often be well expressed in acting to support famine relief and development work, especially where present political structures do not address unmet needs.

The specific policies and measures which agents and agencies must adopt if human potentialities are not to be systematically neglected will also depend, in large part, on the degree of deficiency in the justice of basic institutions. When many populations lack capacities to meet their material needs, or to defend themselves against exploitation and other forms of coercion and deception, the most urgent specific demands of a policy of not neglecting talents and other capacities will lie in the development of basic social and productive skills and institutions that can reduce the weight of injustice. Once again, under circumstances of injustice, many such efforts may be channelled through organizations that work in poor countries and aim to improve literacy, health, farming or other technical skills, or to foster autonomy and self-help. Usually such efforts will not be able to meet all the needs that they confront, or guarantee capacities for autonomous action: but this does not show such action to be ethically inadequate.

Kantian imperfect duties are *selective* obligations. A fundamental maxim of neglecting neither respect nor needed help, nor the development of talents and other capacities, cannot be expressed in a policy of meeting all needs or developing all talents. Respect, since it is mainly a matter of omission, can be universally accorded; beneficence and development of talents and other capacities cannot. This may seem an inadequate account of universal obligations. Should not obligations to meet needs be *unselective*? In particular, how can *selective* beneficence or *selective* development of talents and capacities be justified? For utilitarians and for rights theorists this is indeed a problem. Those who see beneficence as the complete social virtue, as utilitarians do, cannot allow for its selectivity without suggesting that ethical concern may permissibly be local and will surely be unsuited to deliberations on global problems (cf. Singer, 1972; Scheffler, 1982; Kagan, 1984; Goodin, 1985). Yet if such theories hold that beneficence cannot be selective, they face the 'overload of obligations' problem. Rights theorists can indeed see beneficence as legitimately selective, but only at the cost of seeing it as supererogatory, and not a matter of obligation at all. For rights theorists, need drops out of the domain of ethical concern; for utilitarians, it is masked by perceived preferences.

A Kantian account of beneficence avoids these dilemmas because it sees beneficence as a matter of obligation, but not as the whole of a theory of obligation, or even as the central part. Justice is the more fundamental obligation because it concerns the framework of institutions and practices which form the context of action and make certain problems salient, certain solutions possible and certain modes of thought available. However, because it is a matter of structures, justice cannot provide everything that human beings in specific circumstances need to be able to act. Even where material justice is in principle secured, it may be lacking in practice. Amid unjust institutions there is no limit to the needs to which the imperfect obligations of beneficence and development of human potentiality may have to turn to ensure that capacities to act are developed and maintained in all and that the power of social agencies is used to support rather than defeat action by the poor. The selectivity of beneficence and of the development of talents is unavoidable given the unlimited sorts of help and support that human action may need in various circumstances. Although Kantian beneficence and development require only that agents and agencies secure others' capacities for action, and not that they enable them to achieve specific plans or aims, they demand more than any agent or agency can secure for all others. This selectivity is not ethically offensive if imperfect obligations supplement and do not substitute for justice.

5   Justice, Beneficence and Politics

Kantian beneficence may be far from the overload problem in principle; but in a world that is mostly unjust in principle – materially and otherwise – and even more often unjust in practice, it seems that beneficence must be swamped and overcome. Nobody can respond to every need now unmet, nor even to every autonomy-destroying need now unmet. This will seem a disaster if we imagine that beneficence should not only supplement but substitute for a just social order.

In recognizing that selective beneficence is not ethically offensive, we also recognize the prior claims of justice and of political activity in Kantian thinking. Failure to support political activity which, in our actual circumstances, seems likely to help to bring about a more just rather than a less just social order would be a matter of not making a principle of justice fundamental to our lives, policies and practices. Failure to make beneficence do the task of justice is no failure of beneficence. Voluntary and charitable organizations do not fail in *beneficence* if they cannot meet all fundamental material needs, so leaving some still in desperate poverty; nor do the individuals who support them; nor do the individuals who fail to support them, whose beneficence may be committed to other needs or individuals. Each may act with appropriate beneficence; but if these agents and agencies support or buttress a world political and economic system which is an obstacle to material justice, they fail in justice.

This is not to say that every agent or agency should be engaged in 'normal' politics. On the contrary, their engagement in 'normal' politics is their engagement in the politics of the status quo, and so may not help global changes in fundamental political and social structures. 'Normal' political activity is required for justice only when it looks likely to help produce fundamental changes. It is all too easy for agents and agencies who aim for more just institutions to get swallowed up in struggles for budget and project, and in inter-agency rivalry. This can happen even to international and voluntary agencies whose charters and policies commit them to relief of hunger and destitution (McNeill, 1981; Shawcross, 1984). Goals that seemed to lie beyond 'normal' politics may be lost sight of in the course of the struggle. However, sometimes 'normal' political activity can contribute to justice.

In other and harder times established institutional structures may bar such progress. All participation is liable to become collaboration in an unjust status quo. Even here there is nearly always a choice between commitment to a more just future and acquiescence in injustice. Even the most rigid and unjust institutions, the most oppressive collectivities and the most tyrannical individuals, cannot exert total control over action or thought. The very indeterminacy of language means that orders, regulations and actions always remain open to multiple interpretations. No dictator or bureaucracy can do without the judgement – reflective and determinant – of the agents and agencies that it dominates. Even when the range of permissible or possible interpretations is reduced by unjust powers, a stand against forces of darkness is more than personal witnessing or salvation for the soul. It is well understood by oppressed and oppressor that martyrdom is political, but so are many less heroic ways of resisting oppression, not least a refusal to construe the world's problems or their solutions solely in terms of an approved grid of categories. Both individual agents and social agencies can take part in a wider political struggle against unjustice by gradually redrawing the map of political problems and solutions to make injustices salient and their remedy thinkable and ultimately achievable. Such ideological struggle can be *political* only if it remains accessible to those who can act to reduce oppression, and *ethical* only if guided by a view of reasoned deliberation that they can have reason to follow.

There is no incompatibility between beneficent activity aimed at mitigating hunger and poverty, and political activity which has the same end. Agents and agencies who try to limit their action to charity and to be 'nonpolitical', may have good reasons for skirting 'normal' politics (and sometimes they may not). Nevertheless, if they aim to meet those basic human needs whose neglect impedes all action they cannot reject the political aim of finding more just institutions. Justice is not, as utilitarians suggest, merely the most important aspect of beneficence. It is more fundamental than beneficence. A serious commitment to charity and beneficent action requires commitment to material justice and so to political change. Practical reasoning about hunger has an audience only when it reaches those with the power to bring that change.

Note

1   Simone Weil provides a highly suggestive account of these needs and their implications for human obligations in *The Need for Roots*. Her account assumes a theological grounding of obligation.

References

Aiken, William and LaFollette, Hugh (1977), *World Hunger and Moral Obligations*, Prentice Hall, Englewood Cliffs, New Jersey.

Alston, P. (1984), 'International Law and the Human Right to Food', in P. Alston and K. Tomasevski (eds).

Alston, P. and Tomasevski, K. (eds) (1984), *The Right to Food*, Nijhoff, Dordrecht.

Arendt, Hannah (1982), in Ronald Beiner (ed.), *Lectures on Kant's Political Philosophy*, University of Chicago Press, Chicago.

Beiner, Ronald (1983), *Political Judgment*, Methuen, London.

Bentham, Jeremy (1789), *Introduction to the Principle of Morals and of Legislation*, in John Bowring (ed.), 1838–43, *The Works of Jeremy Bentham*, vol. I, reprinted 1962, Russell and Russell, New York.

Bentham, Jeremy (n.d.), *Anarchical Fallacies: being an Examination of the Declarations of Rights issued during the French Revolution*, in John Bowring (ed.), 1838–43, *The Works of Jeremy Bentham*, vol. II, reprinted 1962, Russell and Russell, New York.

Berger, Peter (1974), *Pyramids of Sacrifice: Political Ethics and Social Change*, reprinted 1977, Pelican Books, Harmondsworth, Middlesex.

Boserup, Esther (1981), *Population and Technology*, Blackwell, Oxford.

Bradley, F. H. (1876), *Ethical Studies*, 2nd edn, 1927, Oxford University Press, Oxford.

Brandt, Willy (1980), *North–South: A Programme for Survival*, Pan Books, London ('The Brandt Report').

Brandt, Willy (1983), *Common Crisis North–South: Cooperation for World Recovery*, Pan Books, London.

Brown, Peter and Shue, Henry (eds), (1977), *Food Policy: The Responsibility of the United States in Life and Death Choices*, Free Press, New York.

Brown, Peter and Shue, Henry (eds), (1981), *Boundaries: National Autonomy and Its Limits*, Rowman and Littlefield, Totowa, New Jersey.

Caplan, Arthur L. (1982), 'Mechanics on Duty: The Limitations of a Technical Definition of Moral Expertise for Work in Applied Ethics', *Canadian Journal of Philosophy*, Suppl., vol. VIII, pp. 1–18.

Dinham, Barbara and Hines, Colin (1983), *Agribusiness in Africa*, Earth Resources, London.

Dworkin, Ronald (1977), *Taking Rights Seriously*, Duckworth, London.

Ehrlich, Paul (1971), *The Population Bomb*, Ballantine Books, New York.

Elster, Jon (1982), 'Sour Grapes – Utilitarianism and the Genesis of Wants', in Amartya K. Sen and Bernard Williams (eds), *Beyond Utilitarianism*, Cambridge University Press, Cambridge.

Feinberg, Joel (1979), 'The Nature and Value of Rights', reprinted in Feinberg, Joel (1980), *Rights, Justice and the Bounds of Liberty: Essays in Social Philosophy*, Princeton University Press, Princeton, New Jersey.

Fishkin, James S. (1982), *The Limits of Obligation*, Yale University Press, New Haven.

Frank, A. G. (1969), *Capitalism and Underdevelopment in Latin America*, Monthly Review Press, New York.

Franke, R. W. and Chasin, B. H. (1979), *The Political Economy of Ecological Destruction: Development in the West African Sahel*, Allanheld, Montclair, New Jersey.

French, Peter (1972), *Individual and Collective Responsibility: Massacre at My Lai*, Schenkman, Cambridge, Massachusetts.

Garvey, Terence (1978), *Bones of Contention: An Enquiry into East–West Relations*, Routledge and Kegan Paul, London.

Gellner, E. A. (1983), *Nations and Nationalism*, Blackwell, Oxford.

George, Susan (1984), *Ill Fares the Land: Essays on Food, Hunger and Power*, Institute for Policy Studies, Washington, DC.

Geuss, Raymond (1981), *The Idea of a Critical Theory: Habermas and the Frankfort School*, Cambridge University Press, Cambridge.

Gewirth, Alan (1979), 'Starvation and Human Rights', in Alan Gewirth (1982), *Human Rights: Essays on Justification and Applications*, University of Chicago Press, Chicago.

Goodin, Robert (1985), *Protecting the Vulnerable: A Re-analysis of Our Social Responsibilities*, University of Chicago Press, Chicago.

Guyer, Paul (1979), *Kant and the Claims of Taste*, Harvard University Press, Cambridge, Mass.

Haan, N. de, Bellah, Robert N., Rabinow, Paul and Sullivan, William M. (eds) (1983), *Social Science as Moral Inquiry*, Columbia University Press, New York.

Hampshire, Stuart (1978a), 'Morality and Pessimism', in Stuart Hampshire (ed.), *Public and Private Morality*, Cambridge University Press, Cambridge.

Hampshire, Stuart (1978b), 'Public and Private Morality', in Stuart Hampshire (ed.), *Public and Private Morality*, Cambridge University Press, Cambridge.

Hancock, Graham (1985), *Ethiopia: The Challenge of Hunger*, Gollancz, London.

Hardin, Garrett (1974), 'Lifeboat Ethics: The Case Against Helping the Poor', *Psychology Today*, 8, pp. 38–43 and 123–126; reprinted in W. H. Aiken and H. LaFollette (1977), *World Hunger and Moral Obligation*, Prentice Hall, Englewood Cliffs, New Jersey.

Hare, R. M. (1981), *Moral Thinking: Its Level, Method and Point*, Clarendon Press, Oxford.

Harrison, Paul (1981), *The Third World Tomorrow*, 2nd edn, 1983, Pelican Books, Harmondsworth, Middlesex.

Hartmann, B. and Boyce, J. (1983), *A Quiet Violence*, p. 198, London.

Hinds, S. (1976), 'Relations of Medical Triage to World Famine: A History', in George R. Lucas and Thomas Ogletree (eds), *Lifeboat Ethics: The Moral Dilemmas of World Hunger*, Harper and Row, New York.

Hirsch, F. (1976), *The Social Limits to Growth*, Harvard University Press, Cambridge, Massachusetts.

Höffe, Otfried (1977), 'Kants kategorischer imperativ als kriterium des Sittlichen', *Zeitschrift für philosophische Forschung*, vol. 31, pp. 354–84.

Hoffmann, Stanley (1981), *Duties Beyond Borders: On the Limits and Poss-ibilities of Ethical International Politics*, Syracuse University Press, Syracuse, New York.

IGBA: Independent Group on British Aid, 1983, *Real Aid: A Strategy for Britain*, London.

Jackson, Tony (with Deborah Eade), (1982), *Against the Grain*, Oxfam, Oxford.

Kagan, S. (1984), 'Does Consequentialism Demand Too Much? Recent Work on the Limits of Obligation', *Philosophy and Public Affairs*, vol. 13, 3, 1984, pp. 239–254.

Kamenka, Eugene and Tay, Alice Ehr Soon (1978), *Human Rights*, St Martin, London.

Kant, Immanuel (1781), *Critique of Pure Reason*, trans. N. Kemp Smith, Macmillan, London.

Kant, Immanuel (1785), *Groundwork of the Metaphysic of Morals*, trans. H. J. Paton, 1953, Hutchinson, London.

Kant, Immanuel (1790), *Critique of Judgment*, trans. James Meredith, 1952, Clarendon Press, Oxford.

Kant, Immanuel (1795), 'Perceptual Peace', trans. H. B. Nisbet, in H. Reiss (ed.), *Kant's Political Writings*, 1971, Cambridge University Press, Cambridge.

Kant, Immanuel (1924), *Lectures on Ethics*, trans. Louis Infield, 1963, Harper and Row, New York.

Kitching, G. (1982), *Development and Underdevelopment in Historical Perspective*, Methuen, London.

Lichtenberg, J. (1981), 'National Boundaries and Moral Boundaries: A Cosmopolitan View', in Peter Brown and Henry Shue (eds) (1982).

Lucas, George R. and Ogletree, Thomas (eds) (1976), *Lifeboat Ethics: The Moral Dilemmas of World Hunger*, Harper and Row, New York.

McCloskey, H. J., 1983, *Ecological Ethics and Politics*, Rowman and Littlefield, Totowa, New Jersey.

MacIntyre, Alasdair (1981), *After Virtue: A Study in Moral Theory*, Duckworth, London.

McNeill, D. (1981), *The Contradictions of Foreign Aid*, Croom Helm, London.

Mair, Lucy (1984), *Anthropology and Development*, Macmillan, London.

Malthus, Thomas (1798), *An Essay on the Principle of Population*, reprinted, 1970, Pelican Books, Harmondsworth, Middlesex.

Mamdani, Mahmood (1972), *The Myth of Population Control*, Monthly Review Press, New York.

Martin, Rex and Nickel, James W. (1980), 'I. Recent Work on the Concept of Rights', *American Philosophical Quarterly*, vol. 17, pp. 165–180.

Meadows, Donella H., Meadows, Dennis L., Randers, Jorgen and Behrens, William W., III (1972), *The Limits of Growth: A Report for the Club of Rome's Project on the Predicament of Mankind*, Pan Books, London.

Mill, J. S. (1861), *Utilitarianism*, reprinted in Mary Warnock (ed.) (1962), *John Stuart Mill: Utilitarianism, On Liberty, Essay on Bentham*, Collins, London.

Morgan, Dan (1979), *Merchants of Grain*, Weidenfeld and Nicolson, London.

Nagel, Thomas (1977), 'Poverty and Food: Why Charity Is Not Enough', in Peter Brown and Henry Shue (eds) (1977).

Nozick, Robert (1974), *Anarchy, State and Utopia*, Blackwell, Oxford.

O'Neill, Onora (1975), 'Lifeboat Earth', reprinted in William Aiken and Hugh LaFollette (1977).

O'Neill, Onora (1979), 'The Most Extensive Liberty', *Proceedings of the Aristotelian Society*, pp. 45–59.

O'Neill, Onora (1984a), 'Kant After Virtue', *Inquiry*, 1984, pp. 387–405.

O'Neill, Onora (1984b), 'How to Individuate a Moral Problem', in *Social Policy and Conflict Resolution*, Department of Philosophy, Bowling Green, Ohio.

O'Neill, Onora (1984c), 'Paternalism and Partial Autonomy', *Journal of Medical Ethics*, pp. 173–178.

O'Neill, Onora (1985a), 'The Power of Example', *Philosophy*. (In press.)

O'Neill, Onora (1985b), 'Between Consenting Adults', *Philosophical and Public Affairs*. (In press.)

O'Neill, Onora (1985c), 'Consistency in Action', in Nelson Potter and Mark Timmons (eds), *Morality and Universality: Essays on Ethical Universalizability*, Reidel, Dordrecht. (In press.)

O'Neill, Onora (1985d), 'Rights, Obligations and Needs', *Logos*. (In press.)

Parfit, Derek (1984), *Reasons and Persons*, Clarendon Press, Oxford.

Peguy, Charles (1910), *Victor Marie, Comte Hugo*, reprinted in *Charles Peguy: Oeuvres en Prose, 1909–14*, Gallimard, Paris.

People (1984), August, vol. 11, no. 1, International Planned Parenthood Federation, London.

Rawls, John (1971), *A Theory of Justice*, Harvard University Press, Cambridge, Mass.

Rorty, Richard (1983), 'Method and Morality' in Norma Haan, Robert N. Bellah, Paul Rabinow and William M. Sullivan (eds), *Social Science as Moral Inquiry*, Columbia University Press, New York.

Ruddick, William (1980), 'Philosophy and Public Affairs', *Social Research*, 47, pp. 734–48.

Sahlins, Marshall (1974), *Stone Age Economics*, Tavistock, London.

Scheffler, Samuel (1982), *The Rejection of Consequentialism*, Oxford University Press, Oxford.

Schick, F. (1982), 'Under Which Descriptions?' in Amartya Sen and Bernard Williams (eds).

Schumacher, E. F. (1973), *Small Is Beautiful*, Blond and Briggs, London.

Sen, Amartya, K. (1977), 'Rational Fools: A Critique of the Behavioral Foundations of Economic Theory', *Philosophy and Public Affairs*, 6, 317–344.

Sen, Amartya, K. (1981), *Poverty and Famines: An Essay on Entitlement and Deprivation*, Clarendon Press, Oxford.

Sen, Amartya, K. (1984), 'The Right Not to Be Hungry', in P. Alston and K. Tomasevski (eds).

Sen, Amartya, K. and Williams, Bernard (eds) (1982), *Utilitarianism and Beyond*, Cambridge University Press, Cambridge.

Shawcross, William (1984), *The Quality of Mercy: Cambodia, Holocaust and Modern Conscience*, André Deutsch, London.

Shepherd, Jack (1975), *The Politics of Starvation*, Carnegie Endowment for International Peace, Washington, DC.

Sher, George (1981), 'Ancient Wrongs', *Philosophy and Public Affairs*, pp. 3–17.

Shue, Henry (1980), *Basic Rights: Subsistence, Affluence and US Foreign Policy*, Princeton University Press, Princeton, New Jersey.

Shue, Henry (1981), 'Exporting Hazards', in Peter Brown and Henry Shue (eds).

Shue, Henry (1984), 'The Interdependence of Duties', in P. Alston and K. Tomasevski (eds).

Simon, M. (1957), *Models of Man*, John Wiley and Sons, New York.

Singer, Peter (1972), 'Famine, Affluence and Morality', reprinted 1977 in William Aiken and Hugh LaFollette (eds) (1977).

Singer, Peter (1979), *Practical Ethics*, Cambridge University Press, Cambridge.

Smart, J. J. C. and Williams, Bernard (1973), *Utilitarianism: For and Against*, Cambridge University Press, Cambridge.

Steiner, H. (1974–75), 'Individual Liberty', *Proceedings of the Aristotelian Society*, LXXV, pp. 33–50.

Sumner, L. W. (1981), *Abortion and Moral Theory*, Princeton University Press, Princeton, New Jersey.

Taylor, Charles (1982), 'The Diversity of Goods', in K. Amartya Sen and Bernard Williams (eds), *Utilitarianism and Beyond*, Cambridge University Press, Cambridge.

Verghese, Paul (1976), 'Muddled Metaphors', in George R. Lucas and Thomas Ogletree (eds), *Lifeboat Ethics: The Moral Dilemmas of World Hunger*, Harper and Row, New York.

Wallerstein, Michael (1980), *Food for War, Food for Peace*, MIT Press, Cambridge, Mass.

Walzer, Michael (1977), *Just and Unjust Wars: A Moral Argument with Historical Illustrations*, Basic Books, N.Y.

Walzer, Michael (1981), 'The Distribution of Membership', in Peter Brown and Henry Shue (eds).

Walzer, Michael (1983), *Spheres of Justice: A Defence of Pluralism and Equality*, Martin Robertson, Oxford.

Weil, Simone (1949), *The Need for Roots*, trans. A. F. Wills, 1952, Routledge and Kegan Paul, London.

Wiggins, David (1975–76), 'Deliberation and Practical Reason', *Proceedings of the Aristotelian Society*, LXXVI, pp. 29–51.

Winch, Peter (1958), *The Idea of a Social Science and Its Relation to Philosophy*, Routledge and Kegan Paul, London.

Woodham-Smith, Cecil (1962), *The Great Hunger: Ireland 1845–49*, Hamish-Hamilton, London.

Index

abortion 16, 109, 155–6
abstract reasoning xiv, 4–8, 27–51, 52–6, 62, 68–9, 71–8, 84–5, 93, 97–100, 106, 114–17, 119, 124–8, 130–46. *See* accessibility of ethical reasoning
accessibility of ethical reasoning 27–51, 62, 71–96, 107, 116–20, 121–8, 130–46, 151
accuracy in utility measurement 55, 63–9, 73
action centred reasoning 98–163, *esp.* 118–19, 127, 147
action-guiding reasoning 27–51, *esp.* 47–51, 62, 137
Africa 1, 61
agency xv, 5, 24–6, 29–51, 119–20, 139. *See also* autonomy, collectivities, individualism, institutions, partial autonomy
agent centred reasoning 147
agribusiness 20–1, 122
agricultural surplus 16, 61
agriculture 8, 12–13, 16, 20–2, 60, 62, 65, 112. *See* cash crops, agribusiness, grain
aid 2–3, 24, 55–63, 73–8, 111–13, 151, 153. *See* 'donor' agencies, 'donor' nations
AID (US Agency for International Development) 26n
aid conditionalities 59–63, 73–8
algorithm *see* practical algorithm
allocation of ethical problems 2, 10–26, 125, 144–5. *See* specificatory reasoning, individuation of ethical problems
allocation of obligations 100–3, 144–5
Alston, P. 97, 119, 165
Alston, P. and Tomasevski, K. 101, 113, 118, 119, 120, 145, 165
ancillary principles of action 132, 135, 139, 142
apathy xiii, xv, 67, 153
applied ethics 1–6, 27–51
appropriate technology *see* 'bottom up' initiatives

Archimedean standpoint 46, 98, 127, 133
Arendt, Hannah 143n
Aristotle 29
arms control xiii
artificial persons 35. *See* agency, institutions, collectivities
Asia 1
assimilation to 'normal' ethics 29, 72–82, 97–9. *See* established modes of discourse, 'normal' practical and ethical reasoning
audiences for ethical reasoning 3–6, 27–51, 121–4. *See* accessibility of ethical reasoning
autonomous development 24, 111–12. *See* dependent development
autonomy 36, 65, 106–7, 113–16, 130, 132, 139–42, 146, 149. *See* cognitive capacities, partial autonomy, powers of action

Bangladesh 1, 15, 90, 122
basic needs *see* needs
basic rights 113–16
Beiner, Ronald 29, 31, 143n, 165
beneficence xiv, 2–3, 56–63, 94, 98, 101–4, 108, 126, 139–43, 151. *See* help, obligations of beneficence
benefits 53–7, 63–70, 94, 101, 123, 149
benevolence 133
Bentham, Jeremy 28, 54, 66, 76, 77, 79, 120, 165
Benthamite utilitarians *see* felicific calculus, social science, utilitarian experts
Berger, Peter 9, 10, 11, 87, 88
bias 81–8. *See* neutrality
bilateral aid 22, 60, 74
biological views of hunger 14–19, 26
Boserup, Esther 18, 21, 59, 165
'bottom-up' initiatives 8, 23–4, 60, 112, 153
boundaries xiv, 30–3, 38–51, 86, 90, 115, 117, 119, 121–2, 127, 131, 135–6
Bradley, F. H. 31, 121, 165
Brandt, Willy *see* Brandt Reports

170

DATE DUE